INSIGHT GUIDES

SHOPPING IN
PARIS

Editorial

Series Editor **Cathy Muscat**
Editorial Director **Brian Bell**
Art Director **Klaus Geisler**
Design by **Tanvir Virdee**
Picture Manager **Hilary Genin**
Photographer **Britta Jaschinski**
Cartography **Zoë Goodwin,
Maria Randell**

Distribution

**UK & Ireland
GeoCenter International Ltd**
The Viables Centre, Harrow Way
Basingstoke, Hants RG22 4BJ
Fax: (44) 1256-817988

**United States
Langenscheidt Publishers, Inc.**
46–35 54th Road, Maspeth, NY 11378
Fax: 1 (718) 784-0640

**Canada
Thomas Allen & Son Ltd**
390 Steelcase Road East
Markham, Ontario L3R 1G2
Fax: (1) 905 475-6747

**Worldwide
Apa Publications GmbH & Co.
Verlag KG (Singapore branch)**
38 Joo Koon Road, Singapore 628990
Tel: (65) 6865-1600. Fax: (65) 6861-6438

Printing

Insight Print Services (Pte) Ltd
38 Joo Koon Road, Singapore 628990
Tel: (65) 6865-1600. Fax: (65) 6861-6438

©2003 **Apa Publications GmbH & Co.
Verlag KG (Singapore branch)**
All Rights Reserved
First Edition 2003

CONTACTING THE EDITORS

Although every effort is made to
provide accurate information, we
live in a fast-changing world and
would appreciate it if readers would
call our attention to any errors or
outdated information that may
occur by writing to:

**Insight Guides, P.O. Box 7910,
London SE1 1WE, England.
Fax: (44) 20-7403 0290.
e-mail:
insight@apaguide.demon.co.uk**

ABOUT THIS BOOK

Paris is one of the best cities in the world in which
to spend your hard-earned cash. Its shopping
opportunities are vast, and this guide aims to
offer selected rather than comprehensive listings,
carefully compiled by experts, to help steer you in
the right direction and let you take it from there.

We survey each of the city's main shopping areas,
from upmarket Palais Royal to bohemian Bastille, to
give a flavour of the district and the type of shopping
experience to expect there. A few sightseeing ideas
have been given should you need a retail break. To
help with orientation, each chapter includes an area
map to which the shops are cross-referenced. For ease
of reference the listings are organised by category.

Accompanying the main listings are features on
notable aspects of the Parisian shopping scene, plus
practical tips and ideas on where to relax once your
shopping spree is over. At the beginning of the guide,
we've included a selection of shops that our experts
especially rate, and at the end, you'll find a brief
directory of essential information and an A–Z listing
of all the shops featured.

The authors

The guide was compiled by a team of shop-savvy
journalists, all of whom have spent many years in
Paris: Nicola Mitchell (Champs-Elysées, Saint
Germain, West of Invalides) is an editor and writer
specialising in fashion and lifestyle; Natasha Edwards
(Introduction, Palais Royal, Markets), editor of *Time
Out Paris*, is an art and design specialist, who con-
tributes to many publications both in Paris
and the UK; Joanna Hunter, (Marais,
Bastille) has written for *Time Out*,
The Times and *Elle* magazine among
other publications; Simon Cropper
(Les Halles) and Rosalind Sykes
(Exploring the 16th) are both estab-
lished Paris-based journalists.

Introduction

Shopping Areas

Features

Directory

Maps

For individual zone maps, see area chapters

Le Bon Marché
24 rue de Sèvres, 7th
The slickest, most user-friendly department store in Paris *[p88]*.

La Hune
170 bd Saint-Germain, 6th
A quintessential Left Bank bookstore, La Hune keeps its doors open to bookworms until midnight *[p90]*.

Galeries Lafayette
40 bd Haussmann, 9th
Slowly but surely, this revamped art nouveau department store is regaining its reputation for glamour and abundance *[p38]*.

E. Dehillerin
18 rue Coquillière, 1st
Packed to the rafters with traditional French cookware and kitchen utensils. Every cook's dream *[p54]*.

Colette
213 rue St-Honoré, 1st
Pioneering concept store that picks the best of what is stylish and innovative *[p38]*.

Pierre Hermé
72 rue Bonaparte, 6th
Join the queue for the patisserie king's mouthwatering creations *[p93]*.

Charvet
28 place Vendôme, 1st
This venerable gentleman's outfitters offers a superb choice of ready-made shirts and fabrics for made-to-measure garments *[p35]*.

Galerie Vivienne
6 rue Vivienne, 2nd
The best preserved of all the 19th-century shopping galleries, elegant precursors of the department store *[p44]*.

Barbara Bui
23 rue Etienne Marcel, 1st
'BB' does clean-cut super-smart clothes for the woman about town *[p50]*.

Les Caves Taillevent
199 rue du Faubourg St-Honoré, 8th
A dazzling array of wines with the added bonus of a wine tasting room *[p26]*.

INTRODUCING PARIS

Far from the shopping-mall mayhem of so many cities, the boutiques of Paris make the French capital one of the most relaxing places to shop

When shopping seems to be becoming more and more uniform, with the same international groups and luxury labels in every major city around the world, Paris can still put forward its claim to be the shopping capital of Europe. For one thing, there's an incredible variety of shops in what is a compact, beautiful and easily manageable city. For another, Paris retains its tradition of small specialist shops and personal attention. Although there has been a notable tendancy for fashion labels to try and gain a citywide spread – with Left and Right Bank branches – there seem to be fewer chain stores here than in much of Europe. Thankfully, with the exception of the Forum des Halles and a couple of smaller shopping centres, Paris has remained largely free of the purpose-built *centres commercials* (shopping malls) and the rash of hypermarkets and discount stores that disfigure the Parisian suburbs and the outskirts of many provincial French cities. Instead, individual boutiques ensure that the historic heart of Paris remains a vibrant, living centre.

Opposite: Printemps, a grand art nouveau emporium.

Lie of the land

Luckily, Paris is a relatively easy city to understand. Much of it is comfortably covered on foot – or, alternatively, by means of its efficient bus and metro systems. The most immediately perceptible divide is between the Rive Droite (Right Bank), the traditional centre of business and commerce, and the Rive Gauche (Left Bank), synonymous with intellectuals and learning. The dividing line is the River Seine, which wiggles its way through the heart of the city.

But there is also an east–west divide. Wealthy western Paris is the domain of French aristos and the BCBG ('bon chic, bon genre' – the Parisian equivalent of a Sloane Ranger or Preppy) population who reside in grand Haussmannian residences around the Arc de Triomphe, the Eiffel Tower and in the 'seizième' (16th) district. Poorer eastern Paris is the traditional home of the working-class population, which has been increasingly replaced by immigrant families. But all these divisions have their nuances. Arty centres of creation are now more likely to be in northeast Paris than affluent and unaffordable St-Germain, and young urban professionals are buying into the affordable, traditionally working-class districts.

Administratively, the city is divided into 20 *arrondissements* starting with the 1st *arrondissement* in the centre (taking in part of Ile de la Cité and the area around the Louvre) and spiralling outwards in a clockwise direction to end at the 20th in the northeast. More confusingly, while Parisians often refer to the *arrondissement* where they live – and make all sorts of value judgements about those who live in other *arrondissements* (viz the opposing advocates of the 16th and the 20th) – they also refer to the different, often fuzzy-edged, historic *quartiers*, or districts, such as the Marais, St-Germain-des-Prés, Bastille, Latin Quarter or Ménilmontant, that on occasions divide across *arrondissements* (such as Montparnasse, which falls within bits of the 6th, 14th and 15th), or the Champs-Elysées, an area that takes in more than just the avenue of the name.

Trading places

Historically, Paris's position on the Seine inevitably made it an important trading centre. As early as the 12th century, the Right Bank commerce/Left Bank learning division seems to have been established, with the old market area of Les Halles on one hand and a concentration of medieval schools and religious institutions on the other. Some of these divisions still endure today. Booksellers and publishers still congregate around the Latin Quarter and St-Germain, where the university of Paris has been centred since the middle ages and where printers first set up in the 15th century. Glitzy furniture salerooms and furniture artisans (rather more downmarket today) are still holding out among the bars and fashion stores along the rue du Faubourg-St-Antoine near Bastille. Furniture craftsmen originally gathered here to avoid the restrictions of the medieval trade guilds, their workshops and living quarters clustered around the alleyways that still characterise the area. But if some shopping streets and markets, such as rue Mouffetard and Enfants Rouge, have existed for centuries, many products were originally purchased from itinerant street sellers who cried out their wares.

Printemps and Le Bon Marché, two of the city's first department stores.

In 1789, the French Revolution did more than knock the French king off his throne (and his head from his neck). It also had an effect on the subsequent development of Paris – and consequently shopping. As aristocratic and monastic estates were confiscated by the revolutionary regime, vast new tracts of land came onto the market. One result of this was the boom in covered passages – traffic-free dens hiding emporia filled with all sorts of curiosities. These shopping galleries were forerunners of the department store and many of them have survived, with their old-world atmosphere intact *(see page 44)*.

Paris's population was growing too, bursting beyond Ledoux's 1785 Mur des Fermiers Généraux toll wall that marked the city boundary. In 1860, several former outlying villages including Montmartre, Belleville, Ménilmontant, Charonne, Montrouge, Auteuil and Passy were officially absorbed into the metropolis.

Poîlane's boulangerie, a Parisian favourite.

New residential areas sprang up to accommodate both the flood of migrants coming in from rural France and the populations displaced by Baron Haussmann's grand town-planning schemes in the old city centre. The land architect's broad new avenues may have been partially conceived for keeping down insurrections, but they were also perfect for eye-catching new shopping palaces.

Paris' first department store, Le Bon Marché (lit. good bargain), opened on the Left Bank in 1848. The idea of providing shoppers with an abundant choice of goods at fixed prices in an agreeable setting took off. By the end of the 19th century Le Bon Marché was competing with many other emporia. The grandest of these were Printemps and Galeries Lafayette on the new boulevard Haussmann, just behind the extravagant new Palais Garnier opera house, and La Samaritaine beside the River Seine. With their beautiful domes, mosaics, stained glass and curvaceous metalwork, these Art Nouveau palaces reflected the new prosperity of the age, and showed how shop design was already becoming an important marketing factor.

In the late 19th century, numerous cast-iron market halls were also put up around the city (of which a few, such as the Marché St-Quentin and Marché Beauvau, still exist today), aping the impressive iron pavilions of the central wholesale market at Les Halles. Sadly, the magnificent market halls were razed in the 1970s to make way for the monstrous Forum des Halles, the biggest blot on the Parisian landscape.

What to buy where

Paris's different *quartiers* each have their own mood and atmosphere, and their shops often reflect their history and the type of people who live there. Expect conventional, classic BCBG wear with a fair dose of St-Tropez gilt in Passy; boho designers on the hilly streets of Montmartre; designer couture and an international clientele along avenue Montaigne and Faubourg-St-Honoré; and street-wise streetwear congregated around Les Halles and rue Etienne-Marcel,

minutes from the busy Châtelet-Les Halles public transport interchange through which suburban youth flock into the city. Other areas take a bit more delving: the exclusive residential western sector of the 7th *arrondissement* proves particularly good for city-slicker menswear and equipment for the golfing brigade, along with upmarket interior design boutiques and furnishing fabrics. Although place Vendôme is the place to find sparkly diamond-encrusted baubles, you'll discover more original jewellery designs amid the fine 17th- and 18th-century architecture of Saint-Germain or the Marais. Similarly, if opulent 18th-century antiques are on offer around the quai Voltaire in the 7th and Faubourg St-Honoré in the 8th, you're more likely to spot 1950s and '60s retro furnishing and ceramics near the more alternative Bastille or Montmartre.

However, the geographical shopping map of Paris is far from static, reflecting an ebb and flow that goes with the rise and fall of different *quartiers*. The Champs Elysées, which zigzagged from the epitome of glamour in the early 20th century to that of fast-food tourist dross in the 1980s, returned to favour with a vengeance at the end of the 1990s. Long-staid rue St-Honoré has become the focus for a more avant-garde fashion set, chasing the latest trends at Colette or Maria Luisa. Equally in the past few years, designer fashion has migrated to long-literary St-Germain, to the chagrin of those who bemoan the disappearance of favourite long-standing bookshops and foodstores, although some arrivals such as Karl Lagerfeld's Lagerfeld Gallery have a distinctly Left Bank edge.

If the Marais was first *à la mode* in the early 17th century, when many of its finest aristocratic mansions were built, it subsequently fell into decline with the departure of Louis XIV and his court to Versailles and only began its slow recovery in the 1960s. By the 1990s it was back on top of the desirable areas list. Restoration of its beautiful golden stone *hôtels particuliers* and the installation of important museums such as the Musée Picasso and Musée Cognacq-Jay have turned the Marais into a highly international district and a focus for youthful fashion boutiques and quirky gift shops. A parallel specialist enclave, is the Marais' gay area, the hub of which is around rue Vieille du Temple. The

Kitsch colours at Antoine et Lili.

past few years have seen the arrival of not just bars but gay-oriented book-shops and men's clothing stores, often replacing Jewish bookshops and bakeries in what had long been the main Jewish district.

Other districts also reflect the changing population of Paris. Down in the 13th *arrondissement* 'Chinatown' with its large South-East Asian population, you'll find Chinese supermarkets and *patisseries* among the high-rise tower blocks. Other previously uncharted territories have arrived on the retail map, notably, the Canal St-Martin, where the colourful kitsch Antoine & Lili set up its flagship store.

Other *quartiers* have not fared so well: Les Halles seems to be in perpetual decline with its flagging array of chain stores and dodgy reputation, and the aristocratic past of the boulevards Bonne Nouvelle and Montmartre is a distant memory blurred by the ranks of discount stores and fastfood chains.

Made in France

The fashion industry is still a tangible presence in Paris, from the mass-market sweatshops concentrated around Sentier to the haute-couture houses on Avenue Montaigne. However, French designers no longer dominate the world fashion stage. These days, they share the catwalks with their Italian, British and American counterparts – international stars, transferred like football players between the couture houses in a way that seems to dilute their individuality. But between the couture tags and the high-street chains, you can discover small local boutiques with their own take on French style, street-wise retailers picking out exciting young talents, and the one-off boutiques of individual fashion designers. At a growing number of atelier-boutiques, especially those around the Bastille and Montmartre, you can buy directly from designers and may well see the clothes being made up at the back of the shop.

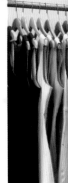

Top: The Champs-Elysées.
Above: Cool Parisian chic at Gaëlle Barré, Bastille.

Other aspects of French design are also worth exploring. Paris has an enviable art and craft tradition, from the classic hallmarks of quality such as Lalique glass, Limoges porcelain and Pierre Frey fabrics to contemporary design gurus such as Philippe Starck, and the rising generation of French designers, including Tsé & Tsé Associés and the Bouroullec brothers, who can be found at outlets such as Edifice or Sentou Galerie.

Then there's food, of course. Paris is a remarkably lived-in city and every *quartier* has its *chocolatiers*, superb *patisseries* and *boulangeries*, delicatessens, ripe-smelling cheese shops and bustling street markets.

Shopping is the perfect excuse for getting to know the city. What better way to appreciate its beauty and character than to window-shop in elegant place Vendôme, meander along the boulevard Saint-Germain, rummage through the book stalls on the banks of the Seine, peer into the eccentric dens of the covered passages, or choose your fruit in the shadow of the Eiffel Tower?

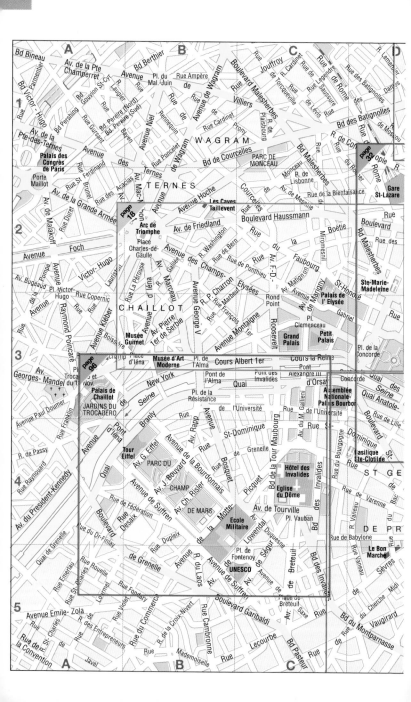

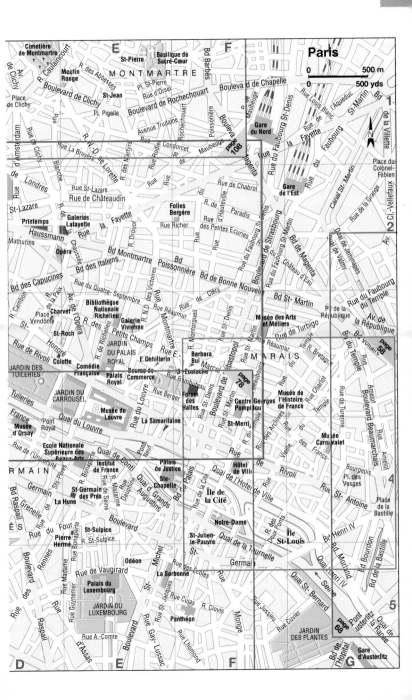

Paris

CHAMPS-ELYSÉES

With a new generation of stylish shops joining the ranks of couture houses and megastores, the Champs-Elysées is making a come-back

The reputation of the Champs-Elysées has ebbed and flowed with the centuries. Visitors anticipating the quintessence of Parisian elegance and charm will be disappointed by the brash commercialism of 'la plus belle avenue du monde'. Its character is defined more by fast-food restaurants, multiplex cinemas, flashy showrooms and global enterprises than pavement cafés and classy boutiques. For a taste of Parisian chic, venture instead to the satellite streets of avenue Montaigne and rue du Faubourg St-Honoré, domain of Parisian haute couture. Here, the fashion houses that line the streets maintain a haughty distance. That said, these days the boundaries between the street-wise and the sophisticates are increasingly blurred. Today the Champs is considered not only elegant again, but a cool place to hang out.

Rise and fall of the 'world's most beautiful avenue'

The avenue was conceived in 1667 when Louis XVI commissioned landscape architect André le Nôtre to extend the perspective of the royal gardens of the Tuileries. Initially, the promenade reached only as far as the Rond-Point des Champs-Elysées. Over a hundred years passed before the rest of the avenue, stretching up to the Arc de Triomphe, was completed. Named after the 'Elysian Fields', the mythological burial ground of the blessed after death, the French version did not live up to the Greeks' sacred ideals. The streets off the Rond-Pont were filled with dance halls that attracted a more profane crowd. Avenue Montaigne, flanking the roundabout, became known as 'Widows' Alley' where bereaved women would seek discreet adventures while officially in mourning.

Opposite: Luxury lingerie from Daniela in Love. Below: Loewe bag.

The Champs' credentials improved greatly after the Arc de Triomphe went up in 1836. The bombastic monument to Napoleon's victories stands at the heart of the star-shaped place de l'Etoile (also known as place Charles de Gaulle), with its 12 sweeping arteries, outlined by Haussmann in 1854. Elegant townhouses began springing up on the upper Champs and surrounding streets, along with grand hotels such as Claridges (at no. 74), cafés and restaurants. The avenue became the essence of chic in terms of fashion, art and gastronomy.

The belle époque was the Champs-Elysées's heyday. One of the few remaining landmarks of that period is the Hotel Païva (no. 25), with its superb onyx stairway. It was the home of Thérèse Lachman, Marquise de la Païva, known for her brilliant literary soirées and progressive views. The marquise would no doubt disapprove of its current proprietor, the Travellers' Club, an institution for misogynist gentlemen.

From the 1950s the avenue filled up with cinemas – Marlene Dietrich lived round the corner on the avenue Montaigne – as well as airline and automobile companies and the headquarters of luxury brands. By the 1970s, though, traffic problems and the

arrival of fast-food chains made it difficult to distinguish the Champs from the main drag of any thriving American city.

The real downturn of the avenue began in 1975 with the decline of Claridge's and the mondaine café, Le Fouquet. For almost two decades Parisians practically disowned the avenue, turning up here only for symbolic occasions, such as New Year's Eve celebrations or memorial services.

The Champs-Elysées ends at the Arc de Triomphe.

The rebirth of cool

It was in 1992 that Jacques Chirac, mayor of Paris at the time, decided to tackle the Champs. He spent 500 million francs (around 75 million euros) building underground car parks to solve traffic congestion, had rows of plane trees planted and newsstands redesigned in belle-époque style. Encouraged by its new look, smart restaurant owners and fashion moguls took a renewed interest in the area. In 1999 a particularly swish branch of the Paris tea salon Ladurée opened at no. 75. Then Louis Vuitton opened a vast store at no. 101. The appearance of Sephora, with its huge array of independent beauty brands and Internet service, attracted the young in-crowd. And now there is Atelier Renault, incorporating a bar, restaurant and exhibition space, in an attempt to put lifestyle ahead of hard sell in the automobile game.

LOCAL ATTRACTIONS

On the north side of the Champs-Elysées, on the corner of avenue de Marigny stands the **Palais de l'Elysée**, official residence of the President of the Republic. On the south side, between place Clemenceau and the river, is the **Grand Palais**, built for the 1900 Exposition Universelle. The spectacular glass-domed central hall is closed for restoration, but two other exhibition areas are used to host prestigious art exhibitions. Its sister building, the **Petit Palais**, has a permanent collection of 19th-century French art, but is closed until 2004. Look out for the **Théâtre des Champs Elysées** (avenue Montaigne) concert hall, worth a visit for the Modernist relief friezes by Rodin's pupil Antoine Bourdelle that decorate the façade and the interior frescoes by Vuillard. And last, but not least, climb to the top of the **Arc de Triomphe** for a fantastic view of the avenue.

Fashionable bars and restaurants have mushroomed in the surrounding streets – Conran's Senso at 16 rue la Trémoille, Pershing Hall at 49 rue Pierre Charron, Tanjia at 23 rue de Ponthieu and star chef Alain Ducasse's world-food bistro Spoon, Food and Wine at 14 rue de Marignan to name but a few.

The shopping streets

The commercial stretch of the Champs-Elysées runs from the Rond-Point (Métro Franklin D. Roosevelt) to the Arc de Triomphe (Métro Charles-de-Gaulle Etoile or George V). The landmark stores are the Virgin Megastore at nos 52–60, where you can sample CDs until midnight; Guerlain at no. 68, with its rococo-style façade and sumptuous interior; the Aladdin's cave of beauty products, Sephora, at no. 70; and Louis Vuitton at no. 101 where queues of wealthy tourists – most of whom are Japanese – wait patiently in line to stock up on gifts (though Vuitton rations the amount they can buy). The majority of the designer shops are concentrated around the avenue Montaigne, avenue George V south, and the rue du Faubourg St-Honoré. This is fashion land, where prices for the majority are prohibitive, but window shopping is free. For a more cutting edge, individual look it's best to head east along the rue St-Honoré.

While fashionistas are well catered for, art devotees won't be disappointed either. Artcurial, an excellent arts bookshop and gallery, can be found at 7 Rond-Point Champs-Elysées, while Christie's France has moved to ultra-smart new premises on avenue Matignon. And don't miss the passageway linking avenue Martigny and rue de Cirque, filled with sumptuous antiques and art galleries. Who cares if the prices are way out of your league, simply feast your eyes on the beauty of these *objets d'art*.

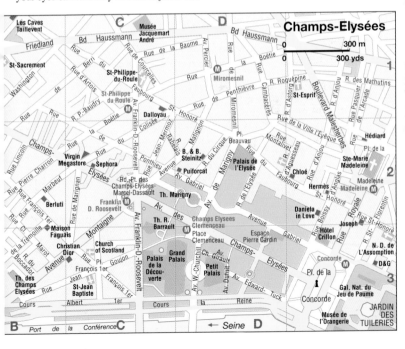

Fashion & Footwear

Alain Figaret

14–14bis rue Marbeuf, 8th [B2]
Tel: 01 47 23 42 86
A Parisian businessman's staple
for crisp cotton shirts and no-fuss
silk ties. They also have a line
of practical, quality separates
in natural fibres for women.
BRANCHES: 16 rue de Sèvres, 6th;
30 avenue Franklin D Roosevelt,
8th; rue de Longchamps, 16th.

Balenciaga

10 avenue George V, 8th [B3]
Tel: 01 47 20 21 11
Head designer Nicolas Ghesquière
has been quietly blowing the dust
off this illustrious fashion house.
The handsome designer who came
from nowhere is now Gucci's hot
property – the group recently
bought Balenciaga.

Berluti

26 rue Marbeuf, 8th [B2]
Tel: 01 43 59 51 10
Present your feet to Olga Berluti,
creative director of Berluti and the
granddaughter of the founder, and
she will define your character as

Classic shoes
from Berluti.

competently as a fortune teller.
Then again, it's not hard to deduce
the type of person who relishes
Berluti shoes with their signature
high sheen and distinctive colour-
ings: rich reds and greens rubbed
into black to create a mirror image.
BRANCH: 171 boulevard Saint-
Germain, 6th.

Camerlo

4 rue Marignan, 8th [C2]
Tel: 01 47 23 77 06
Dany Camerlo's couture caters for
all personalities. The creations of
Russian design duo Seredin et
Vassiliev are definitely for attention
grabbers, while Alberta Ferretti
and Pascal Humbert will suit those
aiming for more subtle seduction.

Céline

36 avenue Montaigne, 8th [C3]
Tel: 01 56 89 07 92
Céline cleverly marries classic
French chic with American sporti-
ness, using the most opulent fabrics.
Affordable to a priveleged few.
BRANCHES: 58 rue de Rennes, 6th;
3 avenue Victor Hugo, 16th.

Chloé

54 rue du Faubourg St-Honoré,
8th [E2] Tel: 01 44 94 33 00
Young British designer, Phoebe
Philo, now wields the scissors at
Chloé, having replaced Stella
McCartney in 2001. Not that things
have changed: clichéd creations of
female eroticism, designed for the
trendy faithful, prevail.

Christian Dior

30 avenue Montaigne, 8th [C3]
Tel: 01 40 73 54 44
Well-heeled mothers, daughters
and granddaughters fill this spacious, fluid store, vacuuming up
flimsy, bias-cut outfits, teetering
talons, gilded cosmetics and
household knick-knacks. More
discreet subversion is rife in the
menswear department where stylish
women are increasingly climbing

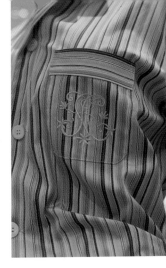

into Hedi Slimane's sleek, severely cut suits. The feminine touch comes from Victoire de Castellane's pretty jewellery for Dior (next door).

BRANCHES: 18 rue de l'Abbaye, 6th; 46 rue du Faubourg St-Honoré, 8th.

Christian Lacroix

26 avenue Montaigne, 8th [B3]
Tel: 01 47 20 68 95

Christian Lacroix's exuberant colours evoke the vibrant palettes of Provençal artists; the designer himself is from Arles. Lacroix's godfather, master embroiderer François Lesage, plays a large part in realising his vision.

BRANCHES: 2 place St-Sulpice, 6th; 73 rue du Faubourg St-Honoré, 8th.

Comme des Garçons

54 rue du Faubourg St-Honoré, 8th [C2] Tel: 01 53 30 27 27

The reclusive designer Rei Kawakubo has at last recognised her mainstream appeal and moved uptown. In her hi-tech 450-m.sq store she offers a different range of gadgets every month. Plus her Comme des Garçons collections.

Daniela in Love...

15 rue Boissy d'Anglas, 8th [E2]
Tel: 01 42 65 02 52

This lovely lingerie boutique attracts businessmen booked into the Crillon across the road either pining for their wives, or hoping to clinch a romantic deal in the city. In-house designer Karine Gilson plays cupid with her custom-made chantilly lace and silk ensembles. Alternatively, impatient lovers can chose from off-the-peg D&G, Roberto Cavalli, Dior and Nina Ricci creations.

Emanuel Ungaro

2 avenue Montaigne, 8th [B3]
Tel: 01 53 57 00 00

Considered *démodé* for some years, Ungaro's work is currently undergoing a new lease of life as a

younger clientele homes in on his intricate, richly coloured designs. The boutique, though, remains as stuffy as a royal box at the opera.

BRANCH: (ready-to-wear) 33 rue de Grenelle, 7th.

Façonnable

9 rue du Faubourg St-Honoré, 8th [E2] Tel: 01 47 42 21 18 04

Façonnable may not be for the hippest dresser, but the menswear chain has everything for a solid achiever's wardrobe from quality business suits to country casuals at reasonable prices.

BRANCHES: 174 bd Saint-Germain, 6th; 27 rue Marbeuf, 8th.

Givenchy

3 & 8 avenue George V, 8th [B3]
Tel: 01 44 31 50 23/01 47 20 81 31

Julien MacDonald's flamboyant designs for his London-based eponymous label have earned him the title of the British Versace, yet his Givenchy look is far more docile. Has the haughtiness of the Paris couture houses cramped his style? Not for long one hopes.

BRANCHES: 28 rue du Faubourg St-Honoré, 8th; 5 rue du Cherche Midi, 6th; (Givenchy Gentleman) 56 rue François 1er, 8th.

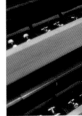

Shirt and cufflinks from Alain Figaret.

The colourful collection of ex-model Inès de la Fressange.

Guy Laroche

28 rue du Faubourg St-Honoré, 8th [E2] Tel: 01 40 06 01 70
Guy Laroche specialised in back surprises, believing that women should be as beautiful leaving a room as entering one. Today, the classic, seductive look prevails.
BRANCH: 9 av Victor Hugo, 16th.

Harel

8 avenue Montaigne, 8th [B3] Tel: 01 47 23 83 03
Harel's classic shoes are unique, timeless, painstakingly crafted and come in many lovely shades.
BRANCH: 7 rue de Tournon, 6th.

Hermès

24 rue du Faubourg St-Honoré, 8th [E2] Tel: 01 40 17 47 10
Old and young fogeys are still well catered for with Hermès' saddle department, horsey-motif scarves, Kelly bags, impeccably tasteful perfumes, John Lobb shoes and discreetly patterned dinner services.
BRANCH: 42 avenue George V, 8th.

Inès de la Fressange

14 avenue Montaigne, 8th [B3] Tel: 01 47 23 08 94
The sunny spirit of ravishing ex-model Inès de la Fressange lives on in this boutique. You'll find colourful poplin shirts, skirts and moccasins, pretty scarves, jewellery and household objects decorated with her signature gold leaf pattern.

Jean Claude Jitrois

40 rue du Faubourg St-Honoré, 8th [E2] Tel: 01 47 42 60 09
Jean Claude Jitrois has been a key name in making leather one of the hottest fashion materials of the moment. He has taken the ultra supple, stretch leather look so far that he will be making nighties in the material soon.

Lanvin

22 rue du Faubourg St Honoré, 8th [E2] Tel: 01 44 71 33 33
Lanvin fashion looks set to recover its gracious look now that Alber Elbaz, fresh from a short stint at Yves Saint Laurent, is designing its womenswear. The men's boutique at no. 15 is a showcase for sartorial elegance, as is the Café Bleue downstairs where sharp-shooting, luxury-goods execs meet for a gossip.

Léonard

48 rue du Faubourg St-Honoré, 8th [E2] Tel: 01 42 65 53 53
This French house with a print heritage is enjoying a comeback. Upbeat designers Michele and Olivier Chatenet are offering jersey dresses either with patterned borders, or full-blown flower patterns over narrow trousers. The result: modern floral chic.
BRANCH: 36 avenue Pierre 1er de Serbie, 8th.

Loewe
54 avenue Montaigne, 8th [C2]
Tel: 01 44 20 84 98
Narciso Rodriguez did an impressive job establishing the fashion line for this Spanish leather-goods company, the result being amazingly supple modern classics. His successor, Enrique Ona Selfa, goes for a funkier, less-uniform look.

Loft Design
12 rue du Faubourg St-Honoré, 8th [E2] Tel: 01 42 65 59 65
The fashion basics offered in this loft-style chain of boutiques are either black, grey or white. Patrick Freche, the brains behind the label, got his inspiration from Paris's winter skyline.
BRANCHES: 56 rue de Rennes, 6th; 175 boulevard Pereire, 17th.

Louis Vuitton
101 avenue Champs-Elysées, 8th [B1] Tel: 01 53 57 24 00
Slip past the snaking queues of tourists making a bee-line for the leather goods and you will eventually spy the sharp, sweetly feminine fashion of Marc Jacobs for the brand. Better still, the LV logo is extremely discreet on the American designer's work.
BRANCHES: 6 place Saint-Germain, 6th; 54 avenue Montaigne, 8th.

Malo
12 avenue Montaigne, 8th [B3] Tel: 01 47 20 26 08
The soft, vibrant shades of Malo's fine cotton and wool separates make a refreshing change from the monochrome displays found in most boutiques on the avenue.

Motsch et Fils
42 avenue George V, 8th [B2] Tel: 01 47 23 79 22
This internationally acclaimed millinery has been creating fabulous men's headgear since 1887. The boutique is worth a visit if only to admire the original mosaic tiled floor and dark wood cabinets.

Paule Ka
45 rue François 1er, 8th [B2] Tel: 01 47 20 76 10
Assured cutter, Serge Cagfinger, is a devotee of the 1950s silhouette, hence his exquisite little black dresses and twin-sets in quality cottons, wools, silks and taffeta. But good taste comes at a price.
BRANCHES: 20 rue Malher; 4th; 192 boulevard Saint-Germain, 6th.

Renaud Pellegrino
14 rue du Faubourg St-Honoré, 8th [E2] Tel: 01 42 65 35 52
Pellegrino's three collections of handbags a year are impeccably finished and unfailingly original. Catherine Deneuve is a regular among his celebrity clients.

Yves Saint Laurent
38 rue du Faubourg St-Honoré, 8th [E2] Tel: 01 42 65 74 59
Since Tom Ford's arrival as head designer, the YSL boutiques have been given a glossy black makeover. Ford's ready-to-wear collections have so far skilfully interpreted the maestro's classics, with sassy up-to-the-minute twists.
BRANCHES: 6 and 12 (men) place St-Sulpice, 6th; 9 rue de Grenelle, 7th; 19 avenue Victor Hugo, 16th.

TIP
Don't be put off buying clothes that don't quite fit. For a small charge, most boutiques offer a 'retouche' or alteration service. But check first whether they can complete the alterations in time for your departure.

Luxury handbags from Loewe.

Pamper yourself with a beauty treatment at the Lancôme Institute or Carlota.

Zenta

6 rue de Marignan, 8th [C2] Tel: 01 42 25 72 47
Zenta's range of sumptuous evening gowns will tempt even the most discreet dresser. The best of the season by Galliano, McQueen, Westwood, Gaultier, Molinari and other top designers.

Health & Beauty

Carita

11 rue du Faubourg St-Honoré, 8th [E2] Tel: 01 44 94 11 29
This cathedral to beauty has been a Parisian landmark since the 1950s. Book a massage or facial treatment, starting with the Rénovateur scrub using Carita's fetish ingredient – sunflower seed oil.
BRANCHES: 39 rue du Cherche Midi, 6th; 3 rue Boccador, 8th.

Carlota

16 avenue Hoche, 8th [B1] Tel: 01 42 89 42 89
Carlota offers highly sophisticated manicures and pedicures. Install yourself in one of the armchairs that heats and massages your body as you enjoy the '1001 Nights' pedicure: a foot bath of rose and jasmine oil, followed by a black soap scrub, another massage, then your toes painted a delicious shade to compliment your designer shoes.

Guerlain

68 avenue des Champs-Elysées, 8th [B2] Tel: 01 45 62 11 21
Visit this belle-époque boutique to appreciate Guerlain's outstanding perfume heritage. Indulge in the superior natural skincare treatments on offer and absorb the beauty of the building itself, constructed in 1913.
BRANCH: 29 rue de Sèvres, 6th.

Lancôme Institut

29 rue du Faubourg St-Honoré, 8th [E2] Tel: 01 42 65 30 74
The prestige beauty brand is indeed an institution, with vast resources for research and development at its disposal, thanks to parent L'Oréal. You can count on being pampered by highly accomplished beauticians armed with the latest miracle-working products.

Makeup For Ever Professional

5 rue La Boétie, 8th [C2] Tel: 01 53 05 93 30
The beauty factory for make-up artists has more than 1,500 products from which to choose.

Parfums Caron

34 avenue Montaigne, 8th [C3] Tel: 01 47 23 40 82

Caron was instrumental in establishing the French perfume industry. Ask to smell *Narcisse Noir* (1911), a favourite of Gloria Swanson, or *Nuit de Noël,* created in 1922 and the inspiration behind 1960s classics *Madame Rochas* and *Calèche*.

Sephora

70 avenue des Champs-Elysées, 8th [C2] Tel: 01 53 93 22 50
For those with a passion for independent beauty brands, a visit to Sephora's cavernous flagship store is essential.
BRANCHES: across Paris.

Design & Interiors

Frette

49 rue du Faubourg St-Honoré, 8th [E2] Tel: 01 42 66 47 70
Although now based in Italy, this distinguished household linen company was founded by Edmund Frette in Grenoble in 1860. Today its superb fabrics still appeal to the French and Italian nobility.

Porthault

18 avenue Montaigne, 8th [B3] Tel: 01 47 20 75 25
Porthault, founded in 1920, only introduced colour into its table linen recently, which shows how seriously it takes its purist image. New technology production methods may now be used for its bed

linen and tablecloths, but the appliqué borders are a homage to traditional craftsmanship.

Puiforcat

48 avenue Gabriel, 8th [D2] Tel: 01 45 63 10 10
The silverware of Jean Puiforcat, who made his name in the 1920s and '30s, will delight art deco fans.
BRANCH: 22 rue François 1er, 8th.

Art & Antiques

Bernard & Benjamin Steinitz

9 rue du Cirque, 8th [D2] Tel: 01 42 89 40 50
This vast antiques gallery, which stretches almost the length of an arcade, has a breathtaking collection of finely crafted objects of the 17th and 18th century. Its forte is boiserie (French wooden panelling) and parquet flooring.

Galerie Lelong

13 rue de Téhéran, 8th [north of C1] Tel: 01 45 63 13 19
Connoisseurs of contemporary art will find the works of major names such as Scully, Tàpies, Andy Goldsworthy and many others in this impressive gallery.

Galerie Segoura

14 place François 1er, 8th [C3] Tel: 01 42 89 20 20
If you have a weakness for French 18th-century art and furnishings,

Beauty product emporium Sephora.

but can't face crowded museums Segoura is a delightful alternative. There are Louis XIV bronzes, paintings by Watteau and Fragonard and priceless porcelain.

La Pendulerie
134 rue Faubourg St Honoré, 8th [C1] Tel: 01 45 61 44 55
Around 200 antique clocks from around the world. Come at noon when these painstakingly restored timepieces chime in unison.

Books, Music & Electronics

Artcurial
7 Rond Pont du Champs Elysées, 8th [C2] Tel: 01 42 99 16 16
This fluidly designed art bookstore and gallery is a pleasant place for browsing, and you can take in their regular exhibitions free of charge.

Fnac
74 avenue des Champs Elysées, 8th [B2] Tel: 01 53 53 64 64
An intrinsic part of French life, Fnac stores stock music, books, computers and photographic equipment.
BRANCHES: across Paris.

Institut Géographique National
107 rue La Boétie, 8th [C2] Tel: 01 43 98 85 00

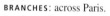

Below: Books and record empire, Fnac.

If you're looking to plan an elaborate holiday route around France complete with gastronomic stopovers, this map shop has all the answers. There are wine, cheese, walking and cycling maps, as well as historic plans of Paris.

Virgin Megastore
52–60 av des Champs Elysées, 8th [C2] Tel: 01 49 53 50 00
Although this store is chaotic, it has a great café with a view of the Champs, and you can sample the latest sounds until midnight.
BRANCH: Carrousel du Louvre, 99 rue de Rivoli, 1st.

Food & Drink

Alléosse
13 rue Poncelet, 17th [north of A1] Tel: 01 46 22 50 45
Supplier to some of the top restaurants around the world, Alléosse has 180–200 cheeses in stock.

Les Caves Taillevent
199 rue du Faubourg St-Honoré, 8th [B1] Tel: 01 45 61 14 09
Taillevent stores some 30,000 bottles in its underground cellar, but this excellent *cave* is not just for connoisseurs. Prices range from stratospheric to the downright cheap. Daily tastings in the Cave du Jour.

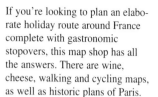

Dalloyau

99–101 rue Faubourg St-Honoré, 8th [C1] Tel: 01 42 99 90 00
Exquisite confectioner and caterer founded in 1802. Specialities include miniature macaroons and a huge variety of chocolate truffles – all packed in cute gift boxes.

Maison Faguais

30 rue de la Trémoille, 8th [B2] Tel: 01 47 20 80 91
Since 1912, three generations of the Faguais family have run this traditional grocery store. It specialises in coffees, jams and condiments.

Paul

49 bis av. Franklin D. Roosevelt, 8th [C2]. Tel: 01 45 61 00 05
This *boulangerie* is full of marvellous breads and pies – the lemon meringue is especially good.
BRANCHES: across Paris.

Specialist

Berthelot

184 rue du Faubourg St-Honoré, 8th [B1]. Tel: 01 45 63 34 07
Artists' supplier and picture framer

in existence since 1852. The paints on sale include the brands Old Holland, Sennelier and Rembrandt.

Mouth-watering creations by Dalloyau.

Elie Bleu

8 rue Boissy d'Anglas, 8th [E2] Tel: 01 47 42 12 21
Hidden away in an arcade, Elie Bleu offers exquisite cigar humidors made in precious woods using traditional cabinet-making methods. Tea caddies and jewellery boxes are also available.

Equistable

177 boulevard Haussmann, 8th [C1] Tel: 01 45 61 02 57
Everything for the horserider and polo player, from saddles and polo sticks to natty shirts and jodhpurs.

WHERE TO UNWIND

Le Cours-la-Reine
Le Cours-la-Reine, off place de la Concorde, is a charming place to escape the hurly burly of the Champs-Elysées. Its three alleys of trees were planted in 1616 by Marie de Médecis.

The Hôtel Plaza Athénée
25 av Montaigne, 8th [B3] Tel: 01 53 67 66 65
In the 18th-century-style Galerie des Gobelins order *mélange Plaza*, a delicious blend of fruit teas, and soak up the old-fashioned luxury.

The Jardins Plein Ciel
17 av Kléber, 16th [A1] Tel: 01 53 64 32 00
The seventh floor of the Hôtel Raphaël offers the most stunning view of the Champs, the Arc de Triomphe and the avenues. Come for

an evening drink when you'll spy the odd celebrity between the potted geraniums.

Ladurée – Salon de Thé
16 rue Royale, 8th [E2] Tel: 01 42 60 21 79
This oh-so-civilised tea room is a Parisian institution and a wonderful place to start the shopping day. Famous for its melt-in-the-mouth macaroons; the *pain au chocolat et pistache* is also a rare treat.

Spoon, Food and Wine
14 rue de Marignan, 8th [C2] Tel: 01 40 76 34 44
Chef Alain Ducasse's inventive dishes are inspired by culinary art and ingredients worldwide and should be experienced at least once.

Hot Couture

Today's creative young designers are using couture as an arena within which they can stretch their creative skills to the limit

When Yves Saint Laurent announced his retirement in July 2002, the French press started another polemic on the demise of haute couture. Predicting the death of made-to-measure has been a regular feature of fashion reporting for the past 40 years. In 1974 *Time* magazine announced that although couture was not actually dead, it was 'breathing very hard'. Its white knight arrived 14 years later in the form of Bernard Arnault, president of the vast LVMH (Louis Vuitton Moët Hennessy) group, which also owns Christian Dior, Donna Karan, Givenchy and Kenzo among others. Arnault financed the launch of Christian Lacroix's couture house, and the fashion editors were delighted – there is nothing like an exuberant collection to animate editorial. The conspicuous consumption of the 1980s fuelled the fascination for couture, but, paradoxically, it was the status that the clothes conferred, rather than their handiwork, that excited buyers. The logo was all, not the look.

Yves Saint Laurent revolutionised the way women dress.

Designer superstars

In the early 1990s Gianni Versace's glitzy creations for pop and movie stars encouraged the phenomenon of the designer as celebrity. Chanel, under the creative direction of Karl Lagerfeld, was the first to exploit couture's new-found sex appeal with the launch of the perfume Coco and accompanying provocative ad campaign. Arnault was also intent on exploiting this logo mania. He hired John Galliano as head designer at Givenchy, when its founder, Hubert de Givenchy, retired in 1995. Two years later he moved the iconoclast to Dior and brought in another British designer, Alexander McQueen, to Givenchy. With Stella McCartney recruited at Chloé about the same time, the Cool Britannia reign was well under way. The threesome threw open the doors of the elitist design studios, letting in street style and a whole jumble of cultural references. The result was huge press coverage and a leap in sales for the LVMH brands' ever- increasing range of accessories, cosmetics and perfumes. The wearability of their couture was not an issue, being such a negligible part of turnover.

So much for couture's revival from a business point of view. On a more creative note, the democratising of high fashion by the *enfants terribles* from across the Channel helped encourage a new generation of designers to take an interest in couture. In 1992, the French Federation of Couture loosened up the rules for establishing a haute-couture house and presenting collections. Today there are 12 official couture houses, and among the most outstanding is Jean-Paul Gaultier, who presented his first couture show in 1987 and has gone from strength to strength ever since. There are also seven 'invited members' of the couture syndicate. Among these are the brilliant Viktor & Rolf, Dominique Sirop, ex-assistant of Hubert de Givenchy, Franck Sorbier who specialises in gowns of hand-painted fabric, the exuberant Korean Ji Haye and techno-charged Maurizio Galante, who sells his intricate designs from his website.

Ironically, it is ready-to-wear that harbours the most promising designers in terms of innovation. The day that Nicolas Ghesquière, currently designer at Balenciaga, or Hedi Slimane, menswear designer for Christian Dior, venture into couture is greatly awaited. Bernard Willhelm, Fred Sathal and Olivier Theyskens are other names to watch. What motivates these designers is a passion for craftsmanship, an urge to keep alive the network of artisans on which couture is based. This unique infrastructure encompassing embroidery, beading, pleating, dyeing and other skills has enabled Paris to remain the fashion capital of the world.

The new couture

It seems that the death of couture has been exaggerated yet again. However, with the departure of Yves Saint Laurent a chapter in its history has certainly come to an end. It's an adieu to fine tuning as practised by Saint Laurent's predecessors, such as Balenciaga and Edouard Molyneux. Like Balenciaga, who closed his couture house in 1967, Saint Laurent retired because he felt his aesthetic was out of sync with the times. 'He sees fashion changing into a game of money and power and it leaves him ill at ease', says his biographer Laurence Benaïm.

Then again, some young fashion professionals see his endless honing of the cut and finish of his 1960s and 1970s classics, which revolutionised the way women dress, as another kind of straitjacket for women. The new couture is about unravelling that impeccable look – with fraying replacing the perfectly finished seam. It's about inventing new codes of design, inspired by the advances in textile technology. Balenciaga, whose catchphrase was 'first the cloth then the couturier', would have approved.

Karl Lagerfeld's little black dress for the Chanel 2003 collection.

Moreover, the new approach coincides with women's preoccupation with individuality and increasing appreciation of quality and style. It's no longer enough to be a heavyweight brand – originality and independence are now fashion bywords. Indeed, couture will never regain its omnipotent role as a dictator of trends; instead it is now an arena for a designer's most innovative and finest work.

As for Yves Saint Laurent, who knows? Perhaps now, freed from the grinding machinations of a multinational, he will find a renewed creative force – watch out for a new label, La Vilaine Lulu – the heroine of cartoons he published in 1967. In any event, his extraordinary vision as a couturier, one that never wavered for 40 years, is likely to go unmatched for a long time, if not for ever.

Looking on the bright side, there is certainly enough couture activity around today to ensure that 'The dark curtain of habit', as Yves Saint Laurent said about designing, 'will not fall.'

PALAIS ROYAL AND THE GRANDS BOULEVARDS

Where venerable institutions rub shoulders with challenging young fashion designers

The area from the Louvre and Palais Royal palaces westwards to the grandiose place de la Concorde, and north to the Eglise de la Madeleine, Palais Garnier and the Grands Boulevards, offers some of the grandest historic buildings and perspectives in Paris and some of the city's smartest shopping to match. But this area is not standing still: long considered rather staid and straight-laced, it has been transformed by the arrival of some of Paris's most desirable and influential boutiques.

Opposite: The little black dress at Didier Ludot. Below: Scent from Shiseido.

In and around the Louvre

The Louvre is not just for art lovers; it can also satisfy the retail needs of fervent shoppers, both in its excellent museum shops and in the underground Carrousel du Louvre shopping centre. The long, arcaded rue de Rivoli runs from the Louvre, along the Tuileries to place de la Concorde. Amid the souvenir shops, the presence of English-language bookshops Gallignani and WH Smith, and shirtmaker Hilditch & Key, are a legacy of the English who often stayed around here in the 19th and early 20th centuries, notably at the Hôtel Meurice, while the arrival of trendy fashion at D&G and concept store-cum-beauty salon Bleu Comme Bleu reflect the trendification of the local fashion scene.

From Concorde, rue Royale (home to legendary art nouveau restaurant Maxim's, elegant tea rooms and the upmarket glass, porcelain and silver manufacturers Lalique, Bernardaud and Christofle) leads to Ste-Marie-Madeleine, a neoclassical church built as a self-aggrandising exercise by Napoleon and a favourite venue for celebrity weddings and funerals. In the square, the mouth-watering displays at foodstores Fauchon and Hédiard are tourist attractions in their own right, but the area also has a concentration of home interiors shops, with branches of Habitat, The Conran Shop, Maison de Famille, Résonances and, for country-house style, Cèdre Rouge. Just off the square, rue Vignon contains several quaint specialist shops and bistros.

Place Vendôme

With a grand vista between the rue de Rivoli and Palais Garnier, octagonal Place Vendôme is perhaps the smartest square in Paris. Laid out in 1699 by Colbert to glorify Louis XIV (whose equestrian statue was subsequently replaced in the centre by a mock-up of Trajan's Column featuring Napoleon's military exploits), it is now occupied by the Hôtel Ritz, the Ministry of Justice and J.P. Morgan bank, and luxury jewellers Chaumet, Van Cleef & Arpels, Bouchardon, Bulgari, Monbuisson and Patek Philippe, and, the most recent addition, Dior. The non-stop array of glittery baubles makes the square a magnet for wishful window-shoppers, though crossing the portals of these heavily guarded domains can be an intimidating experience.

VETIVER ORIENTAL
SERGE LUTENS

SHISEIDO

Rue St-Honoré

The area's commercial heart is the ancient street of rue St-Honoré, which runs parallel to the rue de Rivoli. Once full of noble residences, it still has some elegant façades, such as nos 366–370, and several ornate period shopfronts. However, the area has undergone drastic changes in the past few years, ever since Colette opened here in 1997, setting off the lifestyle-store trend. It has since been joined by Mandarina Duck, Marcel Marongiu, Zadig et Voltaire and arty make-up store Stéphane Marais, making the street a focus for those after the young and original without either the price-tags of the international labels of avenue Montaigne nor the trashier, street bias of rue Etienne-Marcel.

You'll also find little backstreets with small, select boutiques and cafés here. Rue Cambon draws fashionistas for Chanel and the cutting-edge fashion picked out by Maria Luisa. The old covered market at place du Marché-St-Honoré has been replaced by a glass-and-steel complex by Ricardo Bofill. The square houses an interesting range of delis, bistros and boutiques.

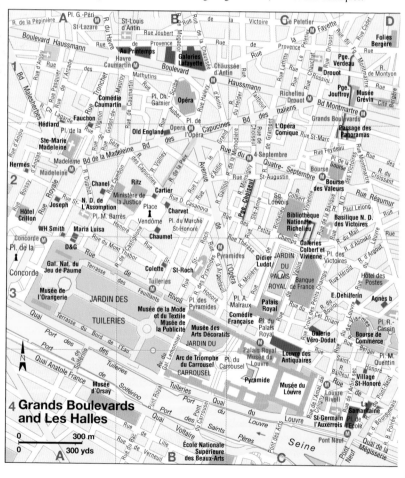

Palais Royal

Palais Royal is a timeless and tranquil spot. The original palace was built in the 1630s but the arcades were added in the 1780s. It's rather more peaceful today than in the early 19th century, when it was notorious for its prostitutes and gambling dens. The palace now contains the Ministry of Culture, while the eccentric mix of shops in the arcades ranges from old-fashioned specialists in medals and lead soldiers to Shiseido make-up, vintage couture and upmarket interior design. The venerable Comédie Française theatre is built into one corner and the neo-rococo Théâtre du Palais-Royal into another, while the haute-cuisine restaurant Le Grand Véfour retains its beautiful period decor.

Rue de Richelieu continues northwards past the old Bibliothèque Nationale and into Paris's main financial district, centred on the Bourse (the French stock exchange), the Banque de France and numerous other banks. The bars and brasseries cater more to businessmen than tourists or shoppers, but it's here that you'll find the covered shopping passages (see p44).

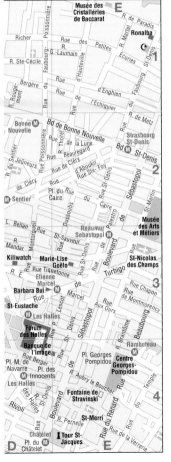

Palais Royal's top sight: the Louvre.

LOCAL ATTRACTIONS

Number one cultural sight is the **Louvre**, a gigantic palace and art museum, with collections that take in Egyptian, Mesopotamian, Greek and Roman antiquities, decorative arts and a superlative collection of European fine art and sculpture from the Middle Ages to the early 19th century. Those interested in fashion should check out the **Musée de la Mode et du Textile**, housed in a separate wing of the Louvre, along with the **Musée de la Publicité** (advertising museum) and the **Musée des Arts Décoratifs**, which is currently undergoing refurbishment. Contemporary art exhibitions are held at the **Jeu de Paume**. For a more relaxing time, take a stroll in the **Jardins du Tuileries** or the **Jardins du Palais-Royal**, while for a sense of grandiose imperial taste, visit **La Madeleine** church and the extravagant **Palais Garnier** opera house.

The Grands Boulevards

North of Palais Royal lie the Grands Boulevards, the string of broad streets that replaced the medieval fortified city wall at the end of the 17th century. The boulevards soon became a place of popular entertainment, lined with restaurants, theatres and later cinemas. Today they are dominated by mass-market clothing chains, discount outlets and chain restaurants, but look up above the plate glass to see some of the fine balconies that remain from when these houses were constructed in the 18th century. North of boulevard Montmartre, the Mairie du IXème on rue Drouot is an elegant *hôtel partic-ulier* that points to this grander past. Behind here, place Drouot is the traditional centre of Paris's secondary art market with auction house Drouot and numerous antiques dealers and valuers. Rue du Faubourg-Montmartre has a busy commercial bustle and is also a focus of the Jewish community, with several kosher restaurants, as well as vintage budget eatery Chartier and nearby Folies Bergère.

At their western end, the Grands Boulevards epitomise the changes under the Second Empire. The sumptuous Palais Garnier opera house, with its ornate sculpted exterior and opulent gilt and polychrome marble interior, was built in the 1860s. In the 1870s and '80s, the area was particularly associated with the Impressionists. Monet, Manet, Caillebotte and Pissarro all painted around here, and the first Impressionist exhibition was held in photographer Nadar's studio on boulevard des Capucines.

Below: On Place Vêndome all that glitters is gold. Right: The shady arcades of Palais Royal.

The end of the 19th century saw the birth of the department store and the on-going rivalry between Galeries Lafayette and Au Printemps as palatial new emporia of fashion and novelties, bringing hitherto unimagined choice to the shoppers who arrived by train. Recently, the department stores have been reinventing themselves, spurred on by the insatiable appetite for designer labels and luxury goods, and the success of lifestyle stores such as Colette. Both Galeries Lafayette and Printemps have gone through major refurbishments in an attempt to win back Parisians, alongside those from the provinces and foreign tourists.

Gentleman's outfitters, Charvet.

Fashion & Footwear

Alice Cadolle
14 rue Cambon, 1st [A2]
Tel: 01 42 60 94 94
The great-grandmother of French corsetry, founded 1889, has a reputation for the perfect fit however generous (or not) your bust. You have to make an appointment for the luxury of a made-to-measure, hand-stitched bra, although there is also a ready-to-wear range.

Apostrophe
23 rue Cambon, 1st [A2]
Tel: 01 42 61 30 81
The sort of wearable, well-made, mid-range womenswear that maintains Parisiennes' reputation for being well-dressed. Lovely soft leather jackets, knitted tops, good-quality classic suits and separates keep in touch with fashion but never leap over the edge.

Cacharel
34 rue Tronchet, 9th [A1]
Tel: 01 47 42 12 61
French clothing group Cacharel has attempted to rediscover its 1970s success with the appointment of hip British duo Clements Ribeiro to oversee design. In have come rejuvenated forms and lots of bright prints. Lines for men, women and children are presented in a light, airy store.

BRANCHES: 64, rue Bonaparte, 6th; 5 place des Victoires, 2nd.

Chanel
31 rue Cambon, 1st [A2]
Tel: 01 42 86 28 00
You can still find the quilted black bag and tailored suit, or Chanel No. 5 (first made in 1921), but the classics are displayed alongside King Karl (Lagerfeld)'s take on sportswear, as he plays games with the Chanel logo on ski pants or frankly silly turquoise tracksuits. The haute couture atelier is still in this building – as is the flat where Coco Chanel once lived.

Charvet
28 place Vendôme, 1st [B2]
Tel: 01 42 60 30 70
Occupying a townhouse on one of the grandest squares in Paris, this venerable gentleman's outfitter is best known for shirts, both ready-to-wear and made-to-measure, but there are also ties, cufflinks, shoes, pyjamas, suits and coats and a small womenswear range.

D & G
244 rue de Rivoli, 1st [A3]
Tel: 01 42 86 00 44
Italian company Dolce e Gabbana's more youthful, streetwise line is shown off in a labyrinthine modern space that suits its relaxed approach. Menswear goes from combat

Did you know?
Gift wrapping is all part of the service expected from a store. Most places in Paris will expertly package your acquisition with suitable frills and ribbons, taking on hordes of students to deal with the Christmas rush.

trousers and kaftan tops to sharp pinstripe suits; for her, a mix of ruffles, punk, stilettos, flat pumps and very cool sunglasses.

Didier Ludot

19, 20, 23, 24 Galerie Montpensier, Palais Royal, 1st [C3] Tel: 01 42 96 06 56
Didier Ludot is the guru of vintage couture with a showbiz clientele that jets in to buy immaculate vintage Chanel, Dior, Balmain or graphic-patterned 1960s Pierre Cardin. There's a boutique devoted to recent creations, including Hermès, Chanel and Prada, while on the other side of the garden, there's a boutique devoted entirely to that little black dress.

Erès

2 rue Tronchet, 8th [A1] Tel: 01 47 42 28 82
The look is generally simple and unflashy but Erès is renowned for Paris's most-flattering swimwear. Bikini tops and bottoms can be purchased in different sizes – or individually. There's also a range of understated lingerie.

Eric Bergère

16 rue de la Sourdière, 1st [B3] Tel: 01 47 03 33 19
Bergère, who began his design career with Hermès, is viewed by many as one of the new designers

capable of reviving the French fashion scene. His womenswear manages to be both feminine and cool – think pointy boots, short skirts and clever detailing – and he also creates impeccably tailored menswear.

Jérôme L'Huillier

27 rue de Valois, Palais Royal, 1st [C3] Tel: 01 49 26 07 07
For those who like dressing up a little, French designer Jérôme L'Huillier produces sexy dresses with a taste for wildly colourful geometric patterns.

Joseph

277 rue St-Honoré, 8th [A2] Tel: 01 53 45 83 32
Joseph Ettegui's vast flagship store, designed with a neo-1970s look by Christian Biecher, is his only Paris outlet to stock men's as well as women's clothes. In the basement, relaxed Joe's Café is set around a glazed bamboo garden.

Lancel

8 place de l'Opéra, 9th [B1] Tel: 01 47 42 37 29
Classic, well-made and pricey – handbags and luggage come in a good range of colours and streamlined shapes.

Madelios

23 bd de la Madeleine, 1st [A2] Tel: 01 53 45 00 00

Try Jérome L'Huillier for that sultry Parisian look.

This vast menswear superstore has taken over most of the old Trois Quartiers shopping centre at Madeleine. Labels include Hugo Boss, Christian Dior, Paul Smith and Versace, ranging from classic suits to flamboyant casual wear, Dunhill and Mont Blanc accessories, plus a beauty salon, café and shoe-shine boys.

Mandarina Duck

219 rue St-Honoré, 1st [B3]
Tel: 01 42 60 76 20
Italian luggage company Mandarina Duck has a hi-tech approach that is reflected in the experimental look of its store. The lightweight, space-age synthetics are applied to clothing as well as handbags and luggage.

Marcel Marongiu

203 rue St-Honoré, 1st [B3]
Tel: 01 49 27 96 38
The Franco-Swedish designer claims his style is rooted in the duality between Latin sensuality and Nordic modesty. He specialises in asymmetric cuts and layering, giving a sophisticated edge to frills and flounces in a range that goes from street-wise separates to swishy silk evening wear.

Maria Luisa

2 rue Cambon, 1st [A2]
Tel: 01 47 03 48 08
One of the hottest multi-label stores in Paris with an eye not only for the avant-garde but for what is wearable. Long-time supporters of John Galliano, Anne Demeulemeester, Martin Margiela and Helmut Lang, but you'll also find rising stars Olivier Theyskens and knitwear whizz Adam Jones. Next door the accessories shop includes Manolo Blahnik and Pierre Hardy shoes, and hats and bags by Philip Treacy; menswear is around the corner in rue du Mont-Thabor.

Jewellery legend, Cartier.

Philippe Model

33 place du Marché-St-Honoré, 1st [B2] Tel: 01 42 96 89 02
If you need a hat to make a statement, then Model is the milliner of choice. Fruit, flowers and feathers adorn his flamboyant creations, which mark Parisian grand occasions – perhaps Chantilly (the French equivalent of Royal Ascot) or a society wedding. You'll also find more sober panamas, and there are shoes and bags too.

Rodolphe Menudier

14 rue de Castiglione, 1st [B3]
Tel: 01 42 60 86 27
Menudier has made shoes for most of the top couture houses and his own luxurious shoe lines – killer heels, sharp boots, etc – are displayed like art works in a striking black and silver boutique by hip young designer Christophe Pillet.

Jewellery/Accessories

Cartier

13 rue de la Paix, 1st [B2]
Tel: 01 42 18 53 70
Although it's now Swiss-owned, Cartier is still the place for glittery diamond sparklers. Perhaps the most desirable item is the square tank watch, produced with variants ever since the 1920s. There's also a selection of vintage pieces.

Cérize

380 rue St-Honoré, 1st [A2]
Tel: 01 42 60 84 84
Witty costume jewellery and accessories displayed in a bonbon-pink, boudoir-like shop. Look out for tiny evening bags from couture embroidery house Lesage and the romantic papier mâché handbags and brooches of Natasha Farina.

Health & Beauty

Comme des Garçons Parfums

23 place du Marché-St-Honoré, 1st [B2] Tel: 01 47 03 15 03
Behind a shocking-pink glass façade, the cool, minimalist interior provides a suitably high-concept setting for CdG's exclusive range of perfumes. Some of them, such as the 'single scent' Leaves range are only available here.

Saponifère

16 rue Vignon, 8th [A2]
Tel: 01 42 65 90 79
The emphasis here is on the bathroom, with everything from soaps, bubble bath and essential oils to pumice stones, towels and badger-hair shaving brushes, but it's also the place to find refined, old-fashioned brands, such as *Creed*, *E Coudray* and *Aqua di Parma*.

Salons du Palais Royal Shiseido

142 Galerie Valois, Palais Royal, 1st [C3] Tel: 01 49 27 09 09
An exquisite setting for the Japanese make-up group and its exclusive scents, such as *Arabie* and *Sa Majesté la Rose*, created by artistic director Serge Lutens.

Department Stores

Colette

213 rue St-Honoré, 1st [B3]
Tel: 01 55 35 33 90
The pioneering concept store surged onto the Paris scene in 1997, not with the department store ideal of colossal choice but with the Colette vision of picking the best of what is stylish and innovative. So far, it has managed to stay ahead of its flock of imitators with its mix of famous names and, as yet, unknowns. You'll find a stool by Tom Dixon, Finnish glasses, a Sony digital camcorder, shoes by Prada, luxury clothes by Tom Ford, and a selection of the hippest CDs and style mags.
The ever-so-chic Water Bar in the basement offers light meals and a global choice of mineral water.

Galeries Lafayette

40 bd Haussmann, 9th [B1]
Tel: 01 42 82 34 56
Galeries Lafayette has restored its art nouveau stained-glass dome and revamped its fashion floors to try and regain the image of glamour and abundance it had in the early 20th century. The fashion choice is colossal, from hip designer labels, such as Isabel Marant, Vivienne Westwood or Prada Sport, and classic womenswear to popular labels, such as Zara and Diab'less, but if you want to check out the up-and-coming take a look at Le Labo and Trends sections on the first floor, which feature innovative young

Colette, the pioneering concept store.

Galerie Lafayette's resplendent art nouveau dome.

designers and with-it accessories. The adjoining Lafayette Homme building has suits, sportswear, men's skincare products, a spa and business centre. Upmarket supermarket Lafayette Gourmet stocks a wide choice of regional and exotic foods, rare *grands crus*, and plenty of opportunities to snack. Late opening on Thursday.

Old England
12 bd des Capucines, 9th [B2]
Tel: 01 47 42 81 99
This *très anglais* department store lives up to the Gallic image of five o'clock tea and city gents in bowler hats. You'll find Floris perfumes, picnic hampers, tea sets, cashmere, Turnbull & Asser shirts, ever-so-traditional children's wear and duffle coats in a rainbow of colours.

Printemps
64 bd Haussmann, 9th [B1]
Tel: 01 42 82 50 00
The eternal rival of Galeries Lafayette has gone seriously upmarket of late. Whereas the Printemps of old seemed to be full of clutter, the revamped version stocks an impressive array of designer fashion and footwear, and even incorporates a Luxe floor, with individually styled mini shops of Gucci, Yves Saint Laurent, Van Cleef & Arpels, etc. In the adjoining Printemps de la Maison,

amid classic porcelain and household linen, a new floor takes a lifestyle look at household objects. Late opening on Thursday.

Design & Interiors

Bernardaud
11 rue Royale, 8th [A2]
Tel: 01 47 42 82 66
The Limoges porcelain house produces both classic dinner services following 18th- and 19th-century patterns, and works by contemporary designers. Look out for the neo-baroque pieces of Robert Le Héros and the elegant stripes of Olivier Gagnère.

Cèdre Rouge
25 rue Duphot, 1st [A2]
Tel: 0142 61 81 81
Cèdre Rouge epitomises French rustic chic for home and garden, with a range that goes from enamelled lava table tops, terracotta pots and stoneware planters to pretty tablewares and glasses, sofas and wrought-iron beds. Closed Monday morning.

Lalique
11 rue Royale, 8th [A2]
Tel: 01 53 05 12 12
Lalique keeps up the glassware tradition of art nouveau master René Lalique with moulded-glass plates, vases and ornaments, often

Did you know?
Coco Chanel's form of wearable chic has made her little wool suit eternal. One of the first to market herself as designer and celebrity, Chanel appeared in photos and magazines and, despite having an apartment above her atelier on rue Cambon, preferred to sleep at the Ritz – all part of the transformation of couturier from humble dressmaker to superstar.

Rustic chic glassware at Cèdre Rouge.

with animal or plant motifs, as well as crystal glasses and jewellery.
BRANCHES: Carrousel du Louvre.

Louvre des Antiquaires
2 place du Palais Royal, 1st [C3] Tel: 01 42 97 29 86
Some 250 upmarket antiques dealers are gathered behind a Haussmannian facade. Specialists take in everything from fine art, porcelain and furniture to Chinese and Japanese ivories, antique jewellery and scientific instruments.

Muriel Grateau
29 rue Valois, Palais Royal, 1st [C3] Tel: 01 40 20 90 30
Grateau's mastery of sophisticated minimalism comes across in the clean lines and subtle colours of smoked-glass tumblers, dark grey plates, luxurious deep-pile towels, and a fabulous range of pure linen place settings and tablecloths available in 100 different colours.

Omio
22–4 rue Boissy d'Anglas/ Village Royale, 8th [A2] Tel: 01 58 18 68 68
An East-meets-West selection of ceramics, homewares and casual clothing which includes Italian linen, Scottish cashmere and tartan-upholstered low chairs, and Japanese ceramics in delicate white porcelain.

Rooming - Périgot
Carrousel du Louvre, 99 rue de Rivoli, 1st [C3] Tel: 01 42 60 10 85
Ingenious inventions for the home and travel come courtesy of Périgot design group. Check out the extendable travelling hangers, snazzy shopping trolleys, flexible plastic wine racks and bottle carriers, assorted mops and brooms and any number of plastic racks, boxes and storage devices.

Books & Music

Brentano's
37 avenue de l'Opéra, 2nd [B3] Tel: 01 42 61 52 50
Brentano's bookshop has a distinctly American flavour, with big sections on business and self-help, as well as all the expected literature, travel and children's books.

La Flute de Pan
49, 53 and 59 rue de Rome, 8th [north of A1] Tel: 01 42 93 65 05
Three shops dedicated to sheet music for all instruments and levels: strings, woodwind, orchestral and learning music at no. 49; brass, percussion and jazz at no. 53; keyboards and vocal at no. 59.

Gallignani
224 rue de Rivoli, 1st [B3] tel: 01 42 60 76 07

Gallignani specialises in glossy art and design books and literature in both English and French, stacked high on mahogany shelves that still give the feel of a bygone era.

WH Smith
248 rue de Rivoli, 1st [A2]
Tel: 01 44 77 88 99
This branch of the British chain has been here for over a century and is always awash with expats and tourists scouring the magazine racks. Open Sunday afternoon.

Gifts & Souvenirs

Musées et Créations
Carrousel du Louvre,
99 rue de Rivoli, 1st [C3]
Tel: 01 40 20 68 84
Crafty items such as glasses, ceramics and silk scarves commissioned from contemporary artists by the state museum organisation. Closed Tuesday.

Nature et Découvertes
Carrousel du Louvre,
99 rue de Rivoli, 1st [C3]
Tel: 01 47 03 47 43
The nature and discovery chain veers curiously between the new age, the nostalgic and the scientific. Still, it's full of original gift ideas from window-sill gardening kits to star-gazing equipment.

Children

Boutique de Floriane
17 rue Tronchet, 9th [A1]
Tel: 01 42 65 25 95
Cute clothes for babies and children come adorned with characters and motifs from the classic French children's stories, Babar the Elephant and Breton nanny Becassine.

Du Pareil au Même
15–17 rue des Mathurins, 8th [B1] Tel: 01 42 66 93 80
This children's clothing chain made its reputation with hardwearing, colourful basics at remarkably low prices, mainly in natural fibres. Note sizes tend to be small.

Le Grand Récré
27 bd Poissonnière, 2nd [D1]
Tel: 01 40 26 12 20
This big brash French toy supermarket chain has a huge choice of all the popular brands, where stereotyping runs true (lots of dolls and mini ironing-boards for girls, guns and cars for boys), plus Lego, Play-Doh, craft sets and the like.

Food & Drink

A la Mère de Famille
35 rue du Fbg-Montmartre, 9th [D1] Tel: 01 47 70 83 69
This *chocolatier* and sweet shop founded in 1761 is almost a museum piece both for its fabulous vintage decor and for the old-fashioned regional sweets and lozenges, such as stuffed Agen prunes, bonbons roses de Reims or les bêtises de Cambrai. Jams and unusual eaux-de-vie, too.

Did you know?

The quitessentially British department store, Old England *(p35)*, was actually founded in 1867 by Frenchman, Alexandre Henriquet, a former salesman at Le Bon Marché.

Psychedelic shopping trolleys at Périgot, Carrousel du Louvre.

Fauchon

26–30 place de la Madeleine,
8th [A2] Tel: 01 47 42 60 11
Although the restaurant sections seem to have encroached on the rest of the shop, Fauchon remains a gourmet destination, with its elegant displays of exotic fruit and veg, fine cheeses, Italian deli, prepared dishes, chocolate and fine wines.

Below and opposite: Gourmet delights from Fauchon and Hédiard.

Hédiard

21 place de la Madeleine, 8th
[A1] Tel: 01 43 12 88 88
In 1854 grocer Ferdinand Hédiard set out to introduce Parisians to new flavours and scents from across the globe. Coffees, teas, spices, dried fruits and nuts remain strong points, along with beautifully packaged jams and honeys, fresh fruit, confits, terrines, wines and prepared dishes.

Legrand Filles et Fils

1 rue de la Banque, 2nd [C2]
Tel: 01 42 60 07 12
This old-fashioned wine merchant has expanded across the Galerie Vivienne *(see p44)* and added a new tasting bar. Although best known for wines from all the French regions, you'll also find chocolate, tea, coffee and wine accessories.

La Maison du Chocolat

8 bd de la Madeleine, 9th [A3]
Tel: 01 47 42 86 52
Chocolatier Robert Linxe has a penchant for combining the dark stuff with exotic flavours and substances such as spices and herbs. One of five elegant Paris branches.

Maison du Miel

24 rue Vignon, 9th [A1]
Tel: 01 47 42 26 70
You can try before you buy at the honey house. The choice of honey takes in all sorts of sources (thyme, oak, etc) and regions both in France and abroad, and there are also bee-related products, such as royal jelly, beeswax, sweets and skin creams.

Maison de la Truffe

19 place de la Madeleine, 8th
[A2] Tel: 01 42 65 53 22
At this temple to the black diamond, you can find the sought-after fungus fresh (November–March), and featuring in oils, sauces and vinegars, as well as its even pricier white cousin from Italy.

Specialist

Bouchara

1 rue La Fayette, 9th [B1]
Tel: 01 42 80 66 95
Bouchara has been in the business of supplying fabrics to Parisians for over a century. Furnishing fabrics, curtain material and brocade are in the basement, table linen and ready-made items on the ground floor, while upstairs dressmaking fabrics go from gingham to raw silk.

Citadium

50–6 rue Caumartin, 9th [B1]
Tel: 01 55 31 73 50
This four-storey sports emporium has latched onto sportswear as much as an urban fashion trend as anything to do with physical exercise. An entire level is devoted to snowboarding, surfing and skateboarding, and there's also kit for football, athletics, golf, hiking and climbing.

Elvis My Happiness

9 rue Notre-Dame des Victoires,
2nd [C2] Tel: 01 49 27 08 43
Records, CDs, videos, Memphis numberplates, posters, magazines, or an Elvis clock with hips that swing with the seconds will guarantee happiness to fans of the King.

Le Prince Jardinier

117 and 121 Galerie Valois, Palais
Royal, 1st [C3] Tel: 01 42 60 37 03
This shop does a range of hand-crafted gardening tools and natural-fibre gardening wear that looks almost too smart to sully outside.

WHERE TO UNWIND

L'Ardoise
28 rue du Mont-Thabor, 1st [A2]
Tel: 01 42 96 28 18
This small, unpretentious bistro tucked between rue de Rivoli and rue St-Honoré, serves modernised French classics and wonderful desserts. Closed Mon and Tues.

Baan-Boran
43 rue Montpensier, 1st [C3]
Tel: 01 40 15 90 45
This hospitable Thai restaurant serves up family-style regional cuisine that varies from fragrant herby salads to fiery red curry.

Café Zéphyr
12 bd Montmartre, 9th [D1]
Tel: 01 47 70 80 14
One of the few cafés with style on the Grands Boulevards. It flanks the entrance of passage Jouffroy, making it an ideal place to lunch.

Hôtel Costes
239 rue St-Honoré, 1st [B2]
Tel: 01 42 44 50 25
For a view of the international fashion and film worlds at play, the Costes' brothers kitsch restaurant is people-watching heaven. Expect trendy world food, skimpy portions, rude staff and a noisy, buzzy atmosphere.

La Ferme Opéra
55–7 rue St-Roch, 1st [B2]
This attractive self-service deli is ideal for a healthy pitstop. Choose from organic salads, sandwiches, fruit juices, cakes and tarts.

In-store eating
Options at Galeries Lafayette include a sushi bar, a smart restaurant and a champagne bar. Not to be outdone, nine restaurants and cafés inside Printemps include Ladurée tea room and the Paul Smith-designed World Bar. The city's smartest delis, Fauchon and Hédiard, both have brasseries and tea rooms, while on rue St-Honoré, the Water Bar at Colette and Joe's Café at Joseph are hip lunch destinations.

Jardins des Tuileries
Stretching between the Louvre and place de la Concorde, the well-manicured Tuileries gardens are the perfect pleasure park: lines of trees, statues, boules players, pony rides, toy boats, cafés and children's trampolines.

Galleries and Passages

*The area between the Palais Royal and rue du Faubourg-Montmartre
is laced with picturesque 19th-century shopping arcades*

The 20 or so shopping arcades, most of which are concentrated around the old Bibliothèque Nationale, represent a fraction of the number that existed in the early 19th century. By the 1840s there were over 100 passages, built by speculators who snapped up the land of the dispossessed aristocracy that came on to the market after the Revolution. They became the places to discover novelties, inventions and the latest fashions, while keeping out of the mud-splashed, carriage-laden thoroughfares. Built with shops below and living quarters above, the glazed roofs testify to the rise of iron-and-glass architecture in these bazaar-like precursors of the modern shopping centre.

Today, although the survivors vary widely in their character between those that have been restored to become fashionable shopping haunts and those that remain humbler reminders of other times, they still have the air of cabinets of curiosities, villagey home to small shops and suppliers, eccentric craftsmen and unlikely specialists that you won't find anywhere else.

Grands galeries

Galerie Vivienne, the most fashionable of all the Parisian galleries.

Just east of Palais-Royal, the **Galerie Véro Dodat** (between 19 rue Jean-Jacques Rousseau and 2 rue du Bouloi), dating from 1826, is perhaps the finest of all the passages, with its wood and brass shopfronts and carved Corinthian capitals. It was constructed as a speculative venture by pork butcher Benoît Véro and his business partner François Dodat. Today, you'll find windows full of antique dolls at Robert Capia, 20th-century collectors' furniture at Eric Philippe and Pascale Drieux, and the handbags and leather goods of Italian company Il Bisonte, as well as the picture-perfect Café de l'Epoque, a good lunch spot.

Thread through the Palais Royal gardens, via the minuscule **Passage des 2 Pavillons** (between 8 rue des Beaujolais and 5 rue des Petits-Champs) to **Galerie Vivienne** (between 4 rue des Petits-Champs, 6 rue Vivienne and 5 rue de la Banque), which has a fine mosaic floor and restored wooden shopfronts. The most fashionable of all the passages, it has been colonised by art galleries and upmarket clothes designers; Jean-Paul Gaultier's haute couture atelier is based here. Oddities include unusual twig and hemp furniture at Bois et Forêts, antique kitchenware at Décor de Cuisine and all sorts of gifts and gadgets at Pylones. Legrand Filles et Fils draws a bankish-set for its wines, while a modish clientele lunches at the A Priori Thé tea room. Adjoining **Galerie Colbert** (6 rue des Petits-Champs, under restoration) has a spectacular glass dome. Formerly an annexe of the Bibliothèque Nationale used for exhibitions, it will hold the future national art history institute.

Petits passages

Further west along rue des Petits-Champs, **Passage Choiseul** (between 40 rue des Petits-Champs and 23 rue St-Augustin) is altogether shabbier, a more prosaic, workaday passage that has seen better days, whose charm lies in its curious array of sandwich shops, discount stores and cheap clothing outlets.

North of the Bourse, the **Passage des Panoramas** (between 10 rue St-Marc and 11 boulevard Montmartre) is one of the earliest of the covered passages. Opened in 1800 on the site of a former aristocratic mansion, Parisians flocked here to see the giant painted panoramas of different cities that were exhibited in two grand rotundas. Stern Graveur has been engraving headed notepaper and wedding invitations since 1840. Look out for the unusual inlaid furniture of Cario Cezkam Atelier with its contemporary take on art deco styling. There are sandwich shops, pizzerias, lingerie at César's, floaty clothes at Sybella, old postcards and vintage vinyl; but above all this passage is a focus for philatelists with half a dozen specialist stamp dealers. Halfway along, the tea room/café L'Arbre à Cannelle occupies an old *chocolatier* with fanciful carved woodwork. The passage itself forms a little network as later, less elaborate offshoots were added in the 1830s, among them the Passage des Variétés, leading to the stage door of Théâtre des Variétés, where Offenbach staged many of his operettas.

Across the busy boulevard, **Passage Jouffroy** (between 10 boulevard Montmartre and 9 rue de la Grange-Batalière) is flanked on one side by the ornate façade of the Musée Grévin, the Paris waxworks museum, and on the other by the soothing Café Zéphyr. Halfway down lies the lace-curtained reception of the old-fashioned Hôtel Chopin. Check out Ciné Doc, where film buffs track down cinema books, specialist reviews and old film stills, the antique silverware at Olivier and an excellent selection of fine and decorative arts books at the Librairie du Passage. There are even two dolls house specialists for those who like their lives miniaturised. The passage continues across rue de la Grange-Batalière as **Passage Verdeau** (between 6 rue de la Grange-Batalière and 31bis rue du Faubourg-Montmartre). A high, airy passage with light streaming through its roof, it has become virtually an annexe of the antique dealers who surround nearby auction house Drouot. Inside the shops, tiny twisty staircases lead up to the apartments above. Here, between a Chinese takeaway, the upmarket Italian deli and wine bar I Golosi, and a shop selling glitzy costume jewellery, you can find vintage cameras, old photographic plates and prints at Photo-Verdeau; 1950s furniture and Vallauris ceramics at Brocéliande; an intriguing mix of antique furniture, sculptures, drawings and tribal art at Le Cabinet des Curieux; outlets for second-hand books and Tintin albums; and rifle through the vintage postcards, meticulously classified in wooden drawers, at La France Ancienne.

Note that most passages are open from around 7am to 9 or 10pm and locked at night and on Sunday. *(The passages around the Sentier area are covered on p49.)*

Mosaic floors and wooden shopfronts of Galerie Vivienne.

Area 3: Les Halles and Sentier

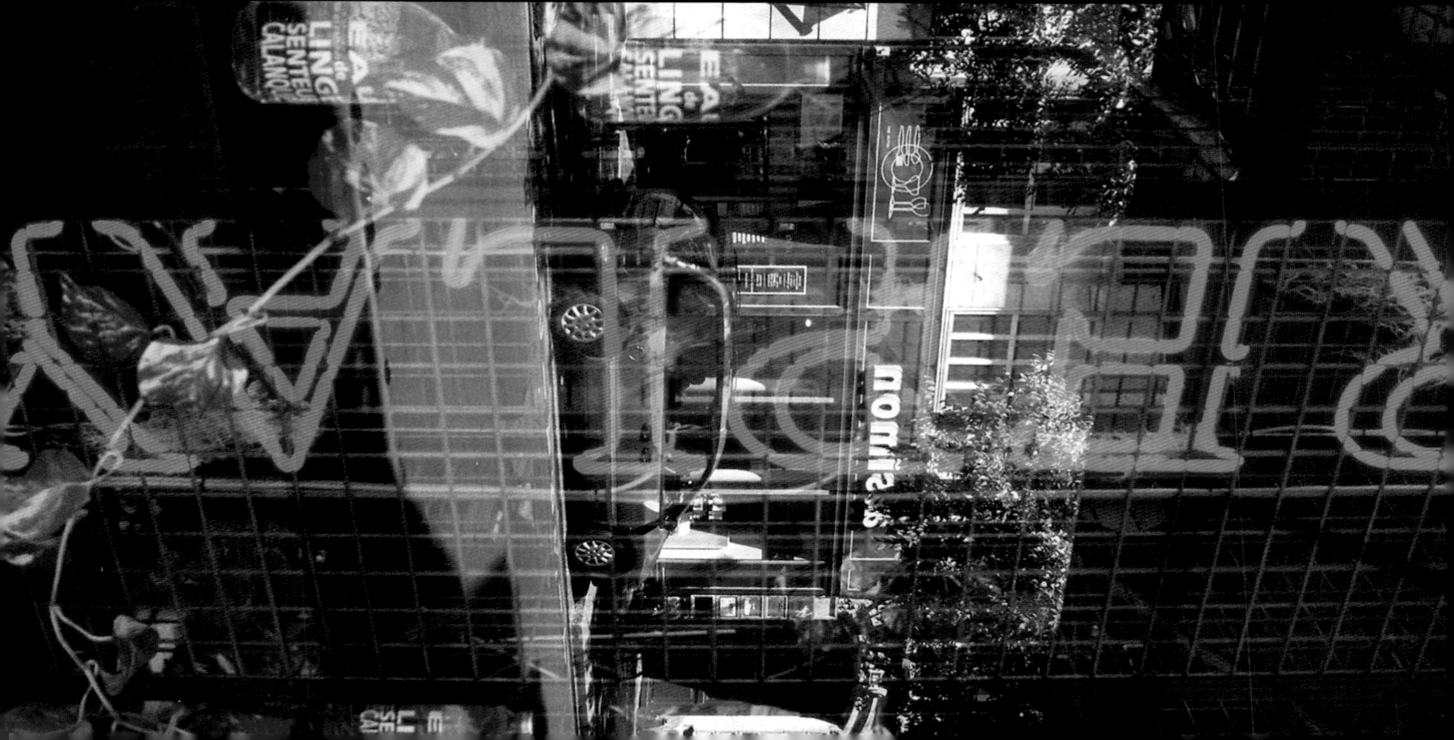

LES HALLES AND SENTIER

The Forum des Halles is devoid of all charm, but the warren of streets around it offer some great bargains and unusual finds

Replay's industrial-look store, for urban cowboys.

Look at a map of the French capital and you'll find Les Halles right in the bullseye. Perhaps surprisingly, this central *quartier* holds few temptations for the average sightseer: no celebrated historic monuments, only minor exhibition spaces (unless you count cinemas) and little picture-book Parisian charm. Immediately to the north, Sentier exerts an even weaker pull on tourists than Les Halles. Don't write them off, though: the two areas aren't wholly lacking in interest and history. Here, it's strictly business, which in Sentier means wholesale clothing and in Les Halles – good news for consumers, if not culture vultures – it's shops, shops and more shops.

The Les Halles quarter gets its name from the city's historic food market, which stood between 1183 and 1969 on the spot now occupied by the biggest shopping complex in Paris. Large-scale construction has been a feature of the site since 1851, when Napoléon III ordered architect Victor Baltard to design ten colossal cast-iron-and-glass hangars to go over the market. By the 1960s the site had become impractical, the market decamped to the suburbs of Rungis, and the hangars were pulled down. With the market gone, the gaping hole had to be filled with something – in the early 1980s, that something turned out to be the Forum des Halles shopping centre (www.forum-des-halles.com).

The Forum des Halles

Four underground levels of shops, two multiplex cinemas, the superb Forum des Images film centre, a gymnasium, an Olympic swimming pool plus direct Métro and RER access mean that in commercial and practical terms the Forum des Halles has nothing to feel embarrassed about. No-one would say the same of its looks. When it went up (or down) the strikingly unlovely Forum was instantly controversial: the above-ground mish-mash of glass, mirrors and white superstructure clashes with the more traditional Paris architecture around it, and the complex quickly earned a reputation as a meeting-point for riff-raff, which has dogged it to this day.

The Forum's focal point is the inhospitable open square three storeys below ground, but the best spot from which to savour the centre's gruesome design is the terrace above street level. A more perilous vantage point can be had in the nearby Jardin des Halles, at the huge skylight that looks some 12 metres (40 feet) straight down onto bustling shoppers: it's accessible to anyone limber enough to hop across the narrow channel of water that separates it from the footpath.

The shops below ground include internationally known brands such as H&M, Habitat and Muji, plus big French chain stores including sports-kit supermarket Go Sport and electronics store Darty. Clothes shops predominate, but with a few exceptions stock only standard-issue fashions.

Cheap 'n' cheerful

Clothes and footwear are even more abundant above the pavement than below, and if the cut-price boutiques don't have something you fancy, maybe the second-hand emporia will: expect to find anything from deafening Hawaiian shirts to aviator jackets and from gypsy dresses to military fatigues. If it's footwear you're after, there are shops that specialise in groovy trainers, cowboy boots (with spurs, should you wish) or walking gear with improbably thick soles. Window-shopping is a piece of cake, as many of the streets in Les Halles are pedestrianised. There are plenty of people-spotting opportunities, too. The crowds – and during business hours the streets are always crowded – reflect the gamut of garments on the racks: swaggering homeboys, pretty young things on the hunt for knock-down 'vintage' attire, tanned men in tight tops and, of course, 'ordinary' guys and gals.

A la Mode

While cheap'n'cheerful reigns supreme in the vicinity of the Forum, things take a modish up-swing along and just off rue Etienne Marcel. Suddenly people seem longer legged, deeper tanned and less socio-economically diverse. Look at the shops, their façades, window displays and price tags, and all becomes clear. (Immutable economic fact: the heftier the price, the smaller the writing on the tag.) It may not have the couture kudos of avenue Montaigne, but if you have a passion for fashion, this is the area your bank manager would like you to avoid. Yohji Yamamoto, Diesel, Joseph and Barbara Bui are just some of the names on the fashion rosary that is rue Etienne Marcel.

South of Les Halles runs genteel rue Saint-Honoré and traffic-laden rue de Rivoli, the latter a run of big French and international brands. Another hop south gets you to the river and the quai de la Mégisserie, which somewhat bizarrely specialises in florists and pet shops.

But for a taste of what Les Halles used to be, make for rue Montorgueil, a narrow pedestrianised street packed with romantic cafés, friendly butchers and colourful fruit 'n'veg stalls. This short strip of charm is one of the few places in Les Halles where it's easy to linger – even if you end up buying nothing more than a coffee.

The Passages

To absorb more of the flavour of old Paris, seek out the passages around Sentier. The original print workshops of the Passage du Caire (off place du Caire), opened 1799, have been replaced by sweatshops, but some of the shopfronts are still adorned with the Egyptian motifs that were the rage after Napoleon's Egyptian campaign. The lofty Passage du Grand-Cerf (between 10 rue Dussoubs and 145 rue St-Denis), has become the home of several design consultancies. With its unusual modern clocks, accessories and retro furniture, As'Art typifies the comeback of the covered passage.

Head north to the Passage Brady (between 46 rue du Faubourg-St-Denis and 43 rue du Faubourg-St-Martin), an outpost of the Indian sub-continent, where you'll find Indian grocers and a succession of colourful curry houses. Nearby, Passage du Prado (between 12 rue du Faubourg-St-Denis and 16 bd St-Denis) is more a part of the Sentier rag trade *(see p55)*. Dating from the 1780s, it was later covered over and redecorated in art deco style. *(For more on galleries and passages see pp44–5.)*

Queen of casual chic Agnès b has colonised the rue du Jour with four shops.

LOCAL ATTRACTIONS

North of the Forum des Halles stands the area's sole architectural gem, the colossal **Eglise Saint-Eustache**. Built in the 16th and 17th centuries, the church has glorious Gothic features, as well as one of the largest organs in France. Even older, the **Tour de Jean-sans-Peur** at 20 rue Etienne-Marcel dates from the 15th century. The tower was part of a fortified feudal keep known as the Hôtel de Bourgogne.

Napoleon's 1798–9 Egyptian campaign is alluded to in the names of several Sentier streets: rue du Caire, rue du Nil, rue d'Alexandrie and rue d'Aboukir. On place du Caire, the façade at no. 2 is decorated with Moorish windows, Egyptian-style hieroglyphics and three large sphinx heads. In the centre just below the eaves is the profile of a man with an enormous nose – said to represent a scoundrel called Bouginier who prowled the area in the early 19th century; the nose and its owner are mentioned in Victor Hugo's *Les Misérables*.

Fashion & Footwear

Agnès b

6 rue du Jour, 1st [D3]
Tel: 01 40 39 96 88
A Parisian fashion institution for stylish clothes at mid-range prices. Famed for her well-cut trousers (especially the leather ones) and sharply but simply styled tops, the French designer has colonised much of rue du Jour: Agnès b enfant at no. 2 for bright and breezy children's wear; Agnès b homme at no. 3, for quality men's separates and Agnès b Voyage at no. 10 for luggage and handbags.
BRANCHES: 13 rue Michelet and 6 rue du Vieux Colombier, 6th; 17 avenue Pierre 1er de Serbie, 16th.

Barbara Bui

23 rue Etienne Marcel, 1st [D3]
Tel: 01 40 26 43 65
With their achingly clean cuts, BB's super-smart garments are the sartorial antithesis of the preponderant Ab-fabbiness along rue Etienne Marcel. Unwind with a Japanese beer at her café at no. 27.
BRANCHES: 43 rue des Francs Bourgeois, 4th; 35 rue de Grenelle, 7th; 50 avenue Montaigne; 8th.

Coming up for air and water outside St Eustache church.

Bill Tornade

44 rue Etienne Marcel, 2nd [D3]
Tel: 01 42 33 66 47
The Bill Tornade label covers men, women and children, but this is the men's store. The snappy urban clothes (lots of black) are hung alongside a sprinkling of square-toed shoes.

Clone

39 rue Etienne Marcel, 1st [D3]
Tel: 01 40 39 92 79
What much of the rest of the street is to legs and shoulders, this groovy boutique is to feet. Shiny shoes and lethal heels abound here. Pricey.

Diesel

35 rue Etienne Marcel, 1st [D3]
Tel: 01 42 21 37 55
Get your motor running… Diesel has three floors of young fashions courtesy of Renzo Rossi. There are glad-rags for men-about-town on the ground floor, and everything for everyone else on the first floor and in the basement.

Espace des Créateurs

Forum des Halles, 1st [D3]
On the first level underground, this run of eight mini boutiques around the sunken square is a refreshing change from the mainstream: dig into women's fashions by Xüly Bet, Yoshi Kando and Futurware Lab.

Kabuki

25 rue Etienne Marcel, 1st [D3]
Tel: 01 42 33 55 65
Kabuki comprises two very fashionable floors – there are bags and shoes by Prada et al at street level, and not-quite-formal-wear by Prada et al on the first.

Kiliwatch

64 rue Tiquetone, 2nd [D3]
Tel: 01 42 21 17 37
Kiliwatch is a huge secondhand shop, specialising mainly in men's and women's clothes from the 1950s to the 1980s. Stock is laid

Cool, understated fashion at Barbara Bui.

out by colour and size, and the most screamingly fashionable items are spotlit. Deeply popular with the cool set, plus the occasional incognito celebrity.

Kookaï
82 rue Réaumur, 2nd [E2]
Tel: 01 45 08 93 69
One of the rare exceptions to the rule that the ordinary punter can't buy clothes in Sentier, this branch of French chain Kookaï is a large, no-frills shop. Reasonably priced, youthful women's fashions are the name of the game, with an unusually wide range of sizes.

Michel Perry
4bis rue des Petits-Pères, 2nd [C3] Tel: 01 42 44 10 07
Michel Perry's shoes for both men and women are smart and classic, with younger, less-expensive styles under the Stephen label. Also displayed in the pink boudoir-style boutique is a small but interesting selection of clothes by the rising young design set including Chloé and Olivier Theyskens.

Naf Naf
4 rue Berger, 1st [E4] Tel: 01 40 39 99 48; 33 rue Etienne Marcel, 1st [D3] Tel: 01 42 36 15 28
Mass-market chain selling affordable fashions for young women. Regular sales and clear-outs provide a steady turnover of bargains.

Replay
36 rue Etienne Marcel, 1st [D3]
Tel: 01 42 33 16 00
Claudio Buziol's industrial-look store features sassy urban togs and plenty of distressed jeans. More radical offshoot E Play is next door.

Jewellery/Accessories

Marie-Lise Goëlo
10 Passage du Grand Cerf, 2nd [E3] Tel: 01 42 36 66 69
The lovely, historic Passage du Grand Cerf is home to some very chic but frankly frivolous boutiques. This is an imaginative exception: a jewellery shop whose entire stock is made from safety pins. The results – diadems, rings, even hats and bustiers – are surprisingly successful.

Lissac
114 rue de Rivoli, 1st [D4]
Tel: 01 44 88 44 44
For groovy shades or even just an extra pair of contacts, this four-storey optician has it all.

Tati Or
57 rue de Rivoli, 1st [E4]
Tel: 01 40 41 03 26
Tati by name, they say, and certainly not in the prestige stratosphere. Still, this jeweller's chain is a good bet for everyday, affordable finery.

TIP

Set in a quiet courtyard, the tiny Village St-Honoré (91 rue St-Honoré) is home to half a dozen pocket-sized boutiques, offering an eclectic array of antiques from Europe, Africa and the Far East.

*Audiovisual
Fnac.*

Department Stores

La Samaritaine

*19 rue de la Monnaie, 1st [D4]
Tel: 01 40 41 20 20*

There's nothing charitable about the prices, but this historic department store with its lovely art nouveau decor certainly covers a lot of shopping territory: textiles, clothing, hardware, toys, you name it. The top-floor Toupary restaurant offers panoramic views over the city.

Design & Interiors

Chez Mamaa

*4 rue Tiquetonne, 2nd [E3]
Tel: 01 40 28 46 09*

Designer watches, lampshades, shelving units, chairs and coffee tables – all dating from the 1960s and '70s – pile up in this wacky, diminutive boutique: just the thing for that Austin Powers interior.

Muji

*Forum des Halles, 18 passage de la Réale, 1st [D3]
Tel: 01 44 88 56 56*

The Japanese no-brand store provides clean-lined merchandise, from cotton bathrobes and slippers to tableware to storage boxes to colouring pencils. Prices are reasonable given the high quality.

Books, Music & Electronics

Fnac

*Forum des Halles,
1 rue Pierre Lescot, 1st [D3]
Tel: 01 40 41 40 00*

The flagship of the Fnac chain is an Aladdin's cave of cultural and technological delights: thousands of books – all at 5 percent off the recommended retail price – in just about every category (even a small English section), CDs and DVDs, audiovisual hardware, computers, software, cameras and photo processing. Avoid it on Saturdays, when it gets oppressively crowded.
BRANCHES: across Paris

Leks

*19 rue Pierre Lescot, 1st [E3]
Tel: 01 40 26 21 83*

This bookshop is great for photography, architecture and design titles – including many in English. Cool contemporary snappers featured include Newton and Araki.

Gifts & Souvenirs

La Banque de l'Image

13 rue de la Cossonnerie, 1st [D4] Tel: 01 45 08 06 41

With racks and racks of postcards outside, the 'image bank' lives up to its name. The postcards tend to be classier than your average Eiffel Tower shots, with plenty by Brassaï, Doisneau et al, plus portraits of artists and writers.

Children

Le Nez de Pinocchio
Forum des Halles, porte Lescot, 1st [D3] Tel: 01 40 26 09 49
This tiny boutique is an unusual phenomenon in the Forum des Halles: a shop with personality. It sells nothing but old-fashioned toys, including wooden train sets or teddy bears that would not have looked out of place in a 19th-century nursery.

Food & Drink

Compagnie Anglaise des Thés
Forum des Halles, 1 rue Pierre Lescot, 1st [D3] Tel: 01 40 39 95 43
Homesick Brits in need of a brew-up can pick up loose-leaf tea at this headily aromatic tea shop. All the standard types of char are here, plus fruit teas and even classy Japanese cast-iron kettles.

Nicolas
59 rue Réaumur, 2nd [E2] Tel: 01 42 36 85 66
The Nicolas wine chain is distinguished for its unfailingly friendly and helpful staff. As well as selling the usual extensive range of wines and spirits, this branch features a wine bar and wine shop.
BRANCHES: across Paris

Pietrement Lambret
58 rue Jean-Jacques Rousseau, 1st [D3] Tel: 01 42 33 30 50
Apart from the large stuffed birds (cockerel and pheasant, etc) in the window, this shop is unassuming, but it sells some first-class foie gras, poultry and game.

Ronalba
54 rue du Faubourg-Saint-Denis, 10th [E1] Tel: 01 44 83 96 30
On the busy ethnic melting-pot that is rue du Faubourg-Saint-Denis, this establishment is one-half deli, full of fabulously pungent French cheeses, 'authentic' lemonades and the like; the other half is a classy wine and spirits store.

Stohrer
51 rue Montorgueil, 2nd [D3] Tel: 01 42 33 38 20
Said to be the oldest *pâtisserie* in Paris (and certainly one of the loveliest), Stohrer has been making and selling exquisite sweet confections for over two and a half centuries.

Left: Le Nez de Pinocchio's best seller. Below: Fnac for music, books and electronics.

Wine and Bubbles
3 rue Française, 1st [D3] Tel: 01 44 76 99 84
The delightfully entitled Wine and Bubbles offers further proof that hipness and English names go hand in hand. This shop sells wines and – *quel surprise* – champagne. They offer a mail order service via their website, and their range includes some extremely exclusive – and expensive tipples indeed: if you're feeling flush and thirsty, you can try a sip of the 1918 Sauternes at 1,524 euros.

E. Dehillerin: an unrivalled selection of traditional kitchenware.

Did you know?

The area around Les Halles makes frequent appearances in 19th-century French literature (Zola set his novel *Le Ventre de Paris* here), and the Baltard halls and workforce were later photographed by such distinguished snappers as Doisneau and Cartier-Bresson.

Specialist

E. Dehillerin

18 rue Coquillière, 1st [D3]
Tel: 01 42 36 53 13

Professional chefs have been coming to this Aladdin's cave for cooks since 1820, and little wonder: with its huge range of knives and copper pans, plus heavy-duty kit like ham-slicers and ice-makers, this is a serious chef's dream.

La Galcante

52 rue de l'Arbre Sec [D4]
Tel: 01 44 77 87 40

This unusual boutique exclusively sells old magazines and periodicals, from 1960s *Paris Match*, *Vogue* and *Elle* (English-language editions included) to humorous French magazines dating from World War I. They also sell 'birthday newspapers'.

Go Sport

Forum des Halles,
1 rue Pierre Lescot, 1st [D3]
Tel: 01 40 13 73 50

From trainers to tennis rackets, bikes, swimming goggles and scuba gear, you'll find equipment and clothing for most mainstream sports in this French chainstore.

A. Simon

48 rue Montmartre, 2nd [D3]
Tel: 01 42 33 71 65

From cocktail sticks to huge copper pans, this famous cookery shop has it all. Don't expect to find much in the way of budget tableware, though: the items on sale are mainly in the 'prestige' bracket, with prices to match.

WHERE TO UNWIND

Au Pied du Cochon

6 rue Coquillière, 1st [D3] Tel: 01 40 13 77 00
In its heyday, the legendary all-night brasserie catered for workers in the food market: now it's rather more upmarket. Famed onion soup.

Flann O'Brien's

6 rue Bailleul, 1st [D4] Tel: 01 42 60 13 58
Guinness aficionados know this Irish watering hole as the home of the smoothest pint of the black in Paris. It's mercifully free of gimmicks and has live music, Wednesdays and weekends.

Le Fumoir

6 rue Amiral de Coligny, 1st [C4]
Tel: 01 42 92 00 24

Subdued lighting and dark wood set the tone for this quietly modish bar. Happy hour is 6–8pm.

Le Grand Rex

1 boulevard Poissonnière, 2nd [D1]
Tel: 08 36 68 05 96
Rest your shopped-out feet while catching a movie on one of the biggest screens in town.

Julien

16 rue du Faubourg-St-Denis, 10th [E1]
Tel: 01 47 70 12 06
This art nouveau brasserie keeps company with the street gamblers just north of Sentier, but the reliable food and magical decor should whisk you away from the hubbub outside.

The Rag Trade

In a pocket just north of Les Halles lies the industrious Sentier district, the hub of the rag trade, where clothes and fortunes are made

Like any area not enshrined in administrative ink, Sentier has fuzzy boundaries; however, in the minds of most Parisians, it is contained by the top right corner of the 2nd *arrondissement*, north of rue Réaumur and east of rue Montmartre. This maze of narrow streets is the undisputed stronghold of the city's wholesale clothes industry – a position it has held since the late 19th century. Though to the outsider Sentier seems jam-packed with clothing and accessory shops, almost all are in fact wholesale showrooms, and few even bother to put up 'Pas de vente au détail' (No retail) signs to make this clear.

Most floors in most buildings are taken over by workshops and storerooms, and in high summer the open windows pour out a constant buzz of bandsaws and sewing machines; but it's at street level that the local colour – textile and ethnic – really comes on strong. Delivery vans block the streets while they unload garish rolls of cloth, and car drivers stuck behind them vent frustration in what locals jocularly refer to as 'car horn concertos'. In the meantime the pace on the pavement is frenetic, as porters from far and wide – North Africans, Pakistanis, Parisians, Chinese, Turks – barrel along with trolleys, cardboard boxes and poles hung with dozens of garments. And yet, because relatively few people actually live in Sentier (a fact reflected in its dearth of bakeries and tobacconists), when work stops for the day, for the weekend or for Jewish holidays, the mayhem fades out to eerie quiet.

Sentier makes clothes, and it also makes fortunes: the sprinkling of Jaguars and Range Rovers are shiny proof of the scale of turnover at the top. The secret to success lies not just in the toil of a low-paid workforce but in the ability of the workshops to take up the latest haute couture trends almost overnight and churn out affordable imitations. But there's also a seamy side to Sentier that has nothing to do with sewing. From time to time police squads swoop on sweat-shops staffed entirely by illegal or semi-legal immigrants, and dodgy dealing is notoriously widespread. And then there's the skin trade on the city's best-known red-light thoroughfare, the rue St-Denis, which features doorway pros-titutes to the north, sex shops and peep shows towards Les Halles.

But though much of Sentier is louche and, to put it mildly, aesthetically nondescript, a few patches are well worth a look: rue Réaumur, with its fas-cinating variety of architectural styles (the result of a series of competitions held between 1898 and 1936); and the passage du Caire and passage du Grand-Cerf *(see p49)*. What's more, there have been growing signs in recent years of a mild shift upmarket, with dotcoms and small media companies moving in among the workshops – and, of course, in some cases folding up and moving out just as fast.

Textiles and garments provide plenty of local colour.

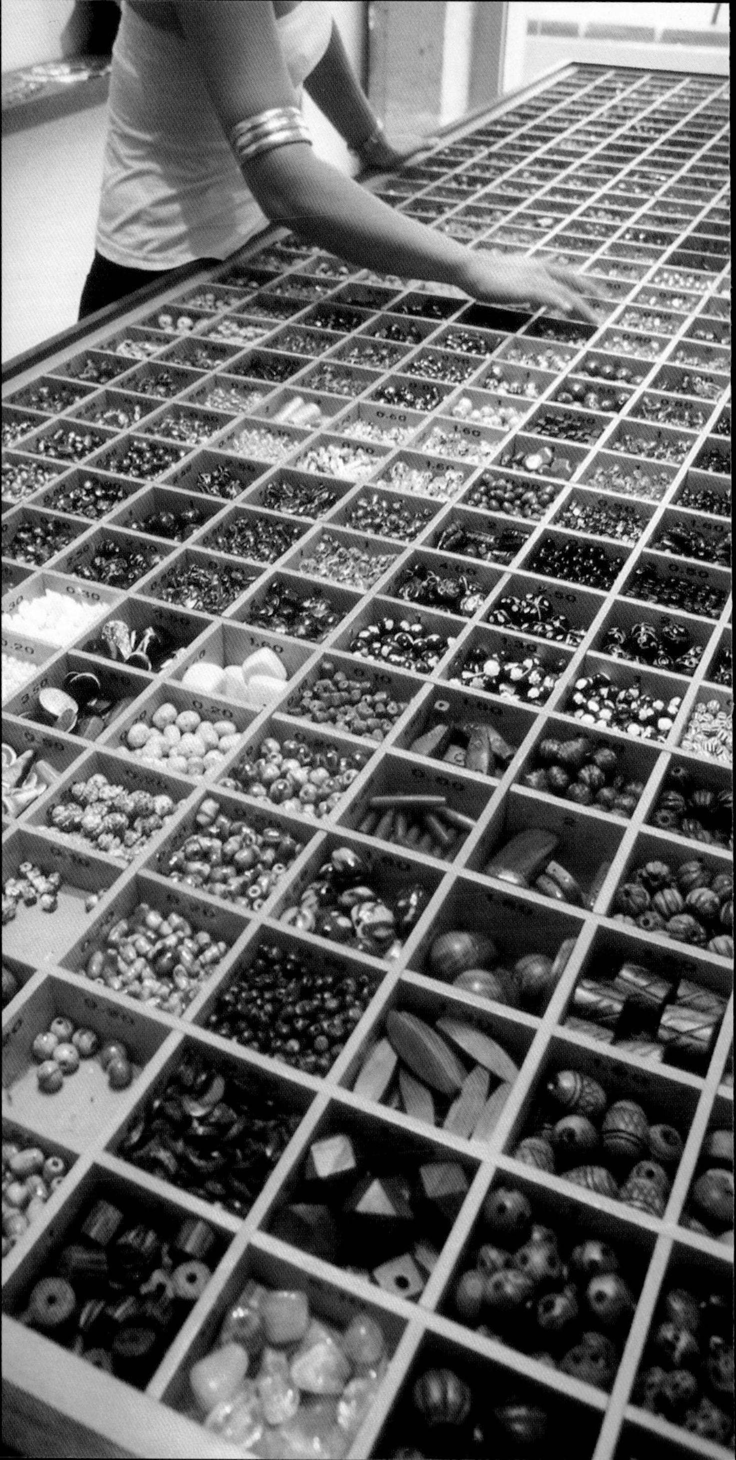

THE MARAIS

Chic boutiques, corner cafés, historic mansions, fashion-conscious residents and a beautiful square – this is Paris in a capsule

There's nowhere quite like the Marais, a district that oozes charm and character with everything to recommend it: mansions and museums, chic boutiques and kosher grocers, gay bars and cosy cafés all bundled together in a labyrinth of narrow streets and alleyways. Stretching west to east from Beaubourg to Bastille, straddling the 3rd and 4th *arrondissements*, with the rue des Francs-Bourgeois pulsing across it like a central artery, the Marais offers arguably the most fun you can have on the Right Bank. And for those of you who can't go a day without shopping, the other important thing to know is that this is one of the few places in the city where you can shop on a Sunday, its busiest and most crowded day of the week.

Opposite: DIY jewellery at Matière Première. Below: Antik Batik, for hippy chic.

In the 17th century, the Marais (literally 'swamp') was transformed from a muddy stretch of farmland into the hub of Parisian high society. The majority of grand and elegant mansions, or *hôtels particuliers,* you see around you date from this period. Then in the 1680s, Louis XIV moved his court to Versailles and the aristocrats left their magnificent homes to follow their king. The area became impoverished and the buildings neglected. It wasn't until the 1960s that renovation began. By the 1990s, the Marais had regained its status as one of the most fashionable – and costly – places to live in Paris. Few of the *hôtels particuliers* are privately owned today. Most of them have been converted into luxury apartments or offices, but a number now house museums *(see box on p59)*.

Place des Vosges and rue des Francs-Bourgeois

A good starting point for your shopping tour is the Place des Vosges. From St-Paul metro station, cross rue St Antoine and head east until you reach the Hôtel de Sully. Walk through the building and cross the lovely courtyard to the back door that exits onto place des Vosges. Built by Henri IV in 1609, this was the first planned square in the city and, with its red brick-and-stone façades tapering into arched walkways, it remains as beautiful as ever.

Apart from the cluster of art galleries at the north eastern end of the square and the eccentric André Bissonnet musical instrument shop on rue Pas de la Mule, there's not much in the way of shopping around the square. The serious shopping begins on the rue des Francs-Bourgeois, which leads off its north-western corner. This stretch, right up to rue Vieille du Temple, is boutique heaven: Antoine et Lili, Barbara Bui, Et Vous, and Mac – they're all here, along with countless little curiosity shops. You'll notice many of the boutiques have retained the shop signs from their previous incarnations as butcher's or baker's; nostalgic reminders of a time when this was a working-class neighbourhood.

Rue des Rosiers

About two thirds of the way down rue des Francs-Bourgeois, look out for the rue Pavée on your left. This leads down to rue des Rosiers, the hub of what remains of the old Jewish quarter. As the area has become increasingly popular with bar and boutique owners, the Jewish community has retreated to a small pocket centred on the rue des Rosiers. Originally an Ashkenazy community, with its origins in eastern Europe, the subsequent influx of Sephardic Jews from north Africa gave the area a Middle Eastern feel.

Among the restaurants and bookshops that surround the synagogue, look for Chez Marianne, the perpetually busy restaurant for Jewish delicacies and *mezes*. For an overview of the area and the people that have lived there, visit the Musée d'Art et d'Histoire du Judaïsme (71 rue du Temple), which looks at the Jewish way of life as well as the history of the Parisian community.

Rue des Rosiers leads on to the rue Vieille du Temple. It has more boutiques but is also one of the best stretches for cafés and bars in Paris.

Beaubourg

The Bazaar de l'Hotel de Ville or BHV (pronounced Bay-Ash-Vay) is a sizeable department store *(see p62)* that marks the dividing line between the Marais and Beaubourg. As department stores go, its selection of goods is

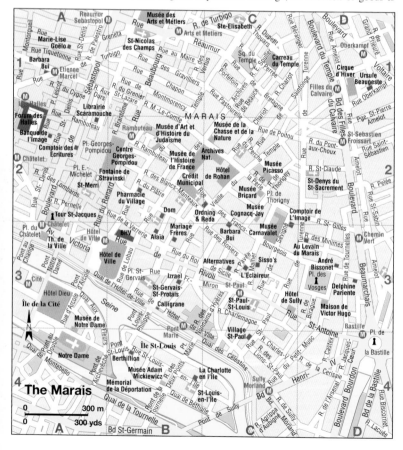

The Marais

unremarkable, but the DIY department in the basement is something else. BHV is also one of the few department stores to hold lists for 'Pacs' – the closest you will come in France to same-sex marriages. The streets around this cornerstone of gay Paris are a sea of rainbow flags and heaving bars.

As you head west in the direction of Beaubourg and Les Halles *(see previous chapter)*, the area gets decidedly sleazy, so keep a weather eye out for pickpockets. Shoppingwise there isn't a great variety here, although there are lots of shops selling arty postcards. The area's most striking feature and major tourist attraction is the Centre Pompidou, the recently revamped modern art museum that opened in 1977 and has been grabbing headlines ever since. The museum is also home to one of Paris's most spectacularly located and stylish restaurants, the Costes brothers' Georges (tel: 01 44 78 47 99).

Ile St-Louis

Leaving the throng behind you, cross the Pont Louis-Philippe to the peaceful haven of Ile St-Louis. Like the Marais, the island was once considered uninhabitable. After Charles V installed a canal that cut right through the middle, it was used for cattle and became known as Ile aux Vaches (Island of Cows). Then, in 1614, Louis XIII decided that the island might be fit for human habitation. The canal was filled in and the island built up with spectacular *hôtels particuliers*.

Today, its quiet streets and spectacular location make it one of the most desirable places to live in Paris. While only a fortunate few can gain access to the beautiful houses, a wander along the rue St-Louis-en-l'Ile, the road that bisects the island lined with gift shops and tea rooms, is the perfect way to take in some of its tranquil charm. And no trip to Paris is complete without paying a visit to the ice-cream experts Berthillon (31, rue St-Louis-en-Ile). There's always a queue, but it's worth the wait.

The Marais streets are a showcase for urban style.

LOCAL ATTRACTIONS

The Marais has more than its fair share of museums, most of which are housed in restored *hôtels particuliers:* the **Musée Carnavalet** (23 rue de Sévigné) traces the history of Paris; the **Musée Picasso** (5 rue de Thorigny) is the artist's personal collection; the **Musée Cognacq-Jay** (8 rue Elzévir) has an exquisite collection of 18th-century *objets d'art;* the **Musée de la Chasse** (60 rue des Archives) has a decorative arts collection celebrating the Hunt; **Musée Bricard** (1 rue de la Perle) is a treasure trove of locks and keys; **Musée du Judaïsme** (71 rue du Temple) covers the art and history of Jewish communities; and on Place des Vosges, **Victor Hugo's former house**, at no. 6, is now a museum dedicated to the life and work of a literary genius.

Fashion & Footwear

Abou Dhabi
10 rue des Francs-Bourgeois, 4th [C3] Tel: 01 42 77 96 98
Gathers the best of the other designer boutiques (Paul et Joe, Isabel Marant, etc) and colour co-ordinates them for us. Ideal for those who like their wardrobes to mix and match.

Alternatives
18 rue du Roi-de-Sicilie, 4th [C3] Tel: 01 42 78 31 50
Alternatives provides surprisingly recent fashion pack cast-offs, including all the big names, for both sexes. Generally in very good condition and often at good rates.

Anatomica
14 rue de Bourg-Tibourg, 4th [B3] Tel: 01 42 74 10 20
Anatomica specialises in straight-forward footwear. Bliss for Birkenstock fans (it's got the whole range of styles and colours) and those who care about being both sartorially and sensibly shod.

Antik Batik
18 rue de Turenne, 3rd [C3] Tel: 01 44 78 02 00
Clothes and accessories with an ethnic influence but by designers who wouldn't think of skimping on luxury and glamour – why else would supermodels wear them? Hippy chic, Parisian style.

Cool boutiques with up-the-minute fashions dominate the Marais.

A-Poc
47 rue des Francs-Bourgeois, 4th [C2] Tel: 01 44 54 07 05
You can tell from the minimal window display that this is high fashion: A-Poc is short for 'a piece of cloth', and designer Issey Miyake is as good as his word. You can cut your own piece of cloth (or have someone do it for you) from great rolls of tubular fabric and it can be turned into anything you like – from a dress to a top, hat or bag. An imaginative approach to designer dressing.

Autour du Monde
12 rue de Francs-Bourgeois, 4th [C3] Tel: 01 42 77 16 18
Boiled wools, bright colours and utilitarian cuts. Get past the pseudo philosophy they like to plaster on the shop windows and you will find simply cut good-quality clothes at a medium price range for both sexes.

Azzedine Alaïa
7 rue de Moussy, 4th [B3] Tel: 01 42 72 19 19
Supermodel favourite and 1980s style-setter Alaïa still designs with the gorgeous and the glamorous in mind. Note that this former warehouse can be tricky to find.

Christophe Lemaire
36 rue de Sévigné, 3rd [C3] Tel: 01 42 74 54 90
Beatnik bobo chic for men and women, firmly rooted in local tradition. The designer also does a sideline in the music that has inspired him, selling CDs and vinyl.

Delphine Pariente
5 rue Pas de la Mule, 3rd [D3] Tel: 01 44 54 95 59
Specialising in all things bright, glittery and gloriously girlie, Delphine Pariente started out with jewellery, but these days her stress is more on clothes and accessories. A firm fashionista favourite.

Issey Miyake, a master of his art.

L'Eclaireur

3 rue des Rosiers, 4th [C3]
Tel: 01 48 87 10 22

One of the most influential boutiques in Paris, L'Eclaireur stocks the big fashion labels (Prada, Jil Sander, Ann Demeulemeester, etc) as well as keeping an eye out for new ones. Ground floor for women, menswear in the basement. See also the loft-style branch with an emphasis on men's clothing at 12 rue Mahler.

Et Vous

6 rue des Francs-Bourgeois, 4th
[C3] Tel: 01 42 71 75 11

Cool and contemporary cuts for the capital's more modish young women. Look for something sexy but stylish at mid-range prices, from sharply cut tops in the softest wool to sequinned flip-flops.

Martin Grant

32 rue des Rosiers, 4th [C3]
Tel: 01 40 28 03 34

An Australian fashion designer in Paris, Grant has lived here long enough to lend his cuts a local slant. Cate Blanchett is one of many fans of his immaculately cut suits and sophisticated dresses.

Plein Sud

21 rue des Francs-Bourgeois, 4th
[C3] Tel: 01 42 72 10 60

For girls who know they're sexy and aren't afraid to show it. The splits are high, the skirts are short, necklines plunging and everything clings in just the right places. But beware – the size range is correspondingly tiny too.

Sisso's

20 rue Mahler, 4th [C3]
Tel: 01 44 61 99 50

Footwear for the ever-so fashionable: but remember those Prada boots weren't made for walking. Sisso's also stocks equally stylish jewellery and accessories.

Jewellery/Accessories

Delphine Charlotte Parmentier

26 rue du Boug-Tibourg, 4th
[B3] Tel: 01 44 54 51 72

One thing you can guarantee about Delphine Charlotte Parmentier's designs is that they'll be dramatic. Extravagant chokers, bracelets and head-dresses made from a variety of unusual materials. Individual commissions also accepted.

La Licorne

38 rue de Sévigné, 3rd [C3]
Tel: 01 48 87 84 43

La Licorne has been making costume jewellery since the 1920s, and continues to sell gems from that era onwards, with an emphasis on bakelite and jet. Be prepared to delve deep to find what you're looking for.

Did you know?
One of the oldest houses in Paris is in the Marais. Built in 1407, no. 51 rue de Montmorency now houses a restaurant – L'Auberge Nicolas Flamel (tel: 01 42 71 77 78).

Les Mots à la Bouche, the largest gay bookstore in Paris.

Matière Première

12 rue de Sévigné, 4th [C3]
Tel: 01 42 78 40 87
If you prefer your jewellery bright and beady, but can't quite find what you're looking for, then why not make it yourself. Thousands of beads to choose from and all the necessary accompaniments.

Health & Beauty

Bains Plus

51 rue des Francs-Bourgeois, 4th [C2] Tel: 01 48 87 83 07
Bath time for big boys: everything a gentleman requires for his *toilette*, from seductive dressing gowns to a good old scrubbing brush.

Dermoplus

31ter rue des Tournelles, 3rd [D3] Tel: 01 44 61 70 00
Beauty house specialising in naturally processed and wonderfully fragranced lotions and potions. Also offers beauty treatments, from facials and manicures to shiatsu.

Lora Lune

22 rue de Bourg-Tibourg, 4th [B3] Tel: 01 48 04 31 23
Almost clinically hygienic, this is the pick 'n' mix of bath products: you can try before you buy, then you pay by the weight. All products are made from natural vegetable oils.

MAC

13 rue des Francs-Bourgeois, 4th [C3] Tel: 01 44 59 31 6
Like a sweet shop for grown ups, big girls can take their pick of this Canadian cosmetic giant's slickly packaged supermodel staples, from lipstick and blusher brushes to a rainbow of nail polishes.

L'Occitane

55 rue St Louis-en-l'Ile, 4th [B4] Tel: 01 40 46 81 71
With its natural products and folksy packaging, L'Occitane is perfect for presents. Soaps, candles, perfumes and bath products, all perfumed with the fragrances of Provence.
BRANCHES: across Paris

Pharmacie du Village

26 rue du Temple, 4th [B2] Tel: 01 42 72 60 71
An ordinary dispensing chemist, but with a local twist: the staff here is gay and can offer advice on subjects such as sexually transmitted diseases and street drugs as well as more orthodox pharmaceuticals.

Department Stores

Bazar de l'Hotel de Ville (BHV)

52–64 rue de Rivoli, 4th [B3] Tel: 01 42 74 90 00
A surprisingly practical oasis in the Marais area, this sizable

department store caters for all things domestic with a strong emphasis on DIY. Popular for wedding lists, gay or straight.

Design & Interiors

Hier Pour Demain
4 rue des Francs-Bourgeois, 4th [C3] Tel: 01 42 78 14 29
'Yesterday for Tomorrow' specialises in furniture and ornaments from the 1920s, '30s and '40s. Period pieces in their original glory or lovingly restored.

Home Autour du Monde
8 rue de Francs-Bourgeois, 4th [C3] Tel: 01 42 77 06 08
The interiors branch of the clothes shop next door. Styles are similarly strong on colour and simple in style. Ground floor is excellent for photo frame-type presents; the basement caters for the boudoir.

Village St-Paul
23–7 rue St-Paul, 3rd [C4]
From Thursday to Monday the area off and around rue St-Paul becomes a warren of antique stalls. Especially good for post-war kitchen items.

Books & Music

Comptoir de L'Image
44 rue de Sévigné, 3rd [C2] Tel: 01 42 72 03 92
Focusing on all things glossy – fashion mags from *Purple* to *Vogue*, old designer catalogues, photographic books – this is a favourite for designers (John Galliano, Marc Jacobs et al) looking for inspiration.

Frédéric Sanchez
5 rue Ste-Anastase, 3rd [C2] Tel: 01 44 54 89 54
Have you ever wondered who compiles the music that makes the fashion shows? Puzzle no more: Sanchez' collection, largely made

up of CDs but including some vinyl, is an eclectic mix from electronica to opera.

Librairie Scaramouche
161 rue St-Martin, 3rd [A2] Tel: 01 48 87 78 58
A nirvana for fans of all things cinematic. The Librairie Scaramouche stocks posters, stills, films and books. There is also a small English-language section.

Les Mots à la Bouche
6 rue Ste-Croix-la-Bretonnerie, 4th [B2] Tel: 01 42 78 88 30
The capital's largest gay bookshop stocks literature from around the world, including an English-language section. This is also an ideal place to find out what's going on in the local gay scene.

Stationery

Calligrane
4–6 rue Pont-Louis-Phillipe, 4th [B3] Tel: 01 48 04 31 89
Those with a passion for paper will be entranced by Calligrane's trio of stores of Luddite luxuries, imported from across the world. Everything is handmade and there are items for a surprisingly wide range of uses, official and domestic.

Comptoir des Ecritures
35 rue Quincampoix, 4th [A2] Tel: 01 42 78 95 10
Ink, pen and paper – Comptoir des Ecriture ensures that the art of calligraphy is far from dead. Its owners even offer courses and exhibitions to prove it.

Ordning & Reda
53 rue Vielle du Temple, 4th [C2] Tel: 01 48 87 86 32
Everything you need to put some order in your life. Reams of paper, notebooks, diaries, etc – all exude that quality of luxury and cheerful efficiency that make Ordning & Reda's stationery so desirable.

Top: Dermoplus for natural beauty products and treatments.
Above: Hier Pour Demain for well restored period pieces.

Kosher shops on rue des Rosiers.

Gifts & Souvenirs

Bernie X
12 rue de Sévigné, 4th [C3]
Tel: 01 44 59 35 88
Look here for art, jewellery, accessories and anything that takes your whim. One of the shop's most famous features is that it changes colour every few months – a quirky little indulgence of the owner.

DOM
21 rue Ste-Croix-de-la-Bretonnerie, 4th [B2] Tel: 01 42 71 08 00
If you like your gifts to be fun – fluffy or inflatable, kitsch or kooky – but generally frivolous, you're certain to find something suitable here. Prepare yourself for the in-house music – it hurts.

Paris Musées
29bis rue des Francs-Bourgeois, 4th [C3] Tel: 01 42 74 13 02
Did you find yourself admiring George Sand's cut glasses, or yearning for a little something by Seurat? This shop offers reproductions from the city-run museums and galleries, as well as works from contemporary designers. It's worth noting that all the museums run by the Mairie de la Ville de Paris (MVP) are free if you want to see the real thing first.

Children

Pylones
57 rue St-Louis-en-L'Ile, 4th [B4]
Tel: 01 46 34 05 02
Wacky, tacky, and kind of fun: you don't have to be a child to shop at Pylones but you do have to have a fondness for rubber jewellery, plastic plants, wind-up toys and Eiffel Tower-shaped ice cubes.
BRANCHES: 13, rue Ste-Croix la Bretonnerie, 4th; 23, bd Madeleine, 1st; 54, Galerie Vivienne, 2nd.

Food & Drink

Au Levain du Marais
32 rue de Turenne, 3rd [D3]
Tel: 01 42 78 07 31
Don't be surprised if there's a queue here: with cakes so beautiful they look like they should be admired rather than eaten, plus Au Levain's speciality organic baguettes, this is the best bakery in the area.

La Charlotte en l'Ile
24 rue St Louis en l'Ile, 4th [B4]
Tel: 01 43 54 25 83
Chocolates, be they bite-size or (literally) statuesque, are the order of the day here. Step further back into the shop and you'll find yourself surrounded by the souvenirs of

a text-book childhood, in La Charlotte's idiosyncratic tea room.

L'Épicerie
51 rue St-Louis-en-L'Ile, 4th [B4]
Tel: 01 43 25 20 14
With almost 100 varieties of jam and a similar number of mustards, a broad selection of oils, vinegars and more sweet treats to follow, L'Epicerie has everything a gourmet might wish for. Prettily packaged too.

Finkelsztajn
27 rue des Rosiers, 4th [C3]
Tel: 01 42 72 78 91
Abandon all diets before you enter: the area's Jewish influence is evident in a sumptuous array of kosher cakes with a strong emphasis on apple and cream cheese.

Izraël
30 rue François-Miron, 4th [B3]
Tel: 01 42 72 66 23
Don't be fooled by the name – the delicacies that fill every shelf, corner and other bit of available floor space are by no means restricted to the Middle East. Cheeses, cakes, pulses, nuts, olives and oils, from Mexico to the Maghreb.

Mariage Frères
30 rue du Bourg-Tibourg, 4th [B3] Tel 01 42 72 28 11
Some 500 types of tea, accompanied by pots, cups and every other tea-time accessory you could imagine. But be warned – serving suggestions verge on the scientific. If you want to try before you buy, get yourself to the shop's tea room.

Specialist

Argenterie de Turenne
19 rue de Turenne, 3rd [C3]
Tel: 01 42 72 04 00
Specialising in all things silver, the selection here is largely French and from the late 19th to early 20th century. Look out for the silver-plated cutlery sold by the gram.

André Bissonnet
6 rue Pas de la Mule, 3rd [D3]
Tel: 01 48 87 20 15
A glance through the window at the packed interior gives the game away: André Bissonet buys and sells old musical instruments, from violins to percussion instruments, all in excellent condition.

WHERE TO UNWIND

Au Petit Fer à Cheval
30 rue Vieille-du-Temple, 4th [C2]
Tel: 01 42 72 47 47
People-watching is as much a full-time occupation here as it is in the rest of Paris – or indeed anywhere else along the rue Vieille-du-Temple. With its tiny horseshoe-shaped bar, this café is, however, particularly atmospheric

Les Bains du Marais
31–3 rue des Blancs-Manteaux, 3rd [B2]
Tel: 01 44 61 02 02
For some dedicated relaxation, try this modern take on the traditional hammam, complete with steam room and café. Les Bains also offers facial treatments and massages.

Café Beaubourg
43 rue St-Merri, 4th [B2] Tel: 01 48 87 63 96
Either gaze out from the terrace onto the forecourt of the Centre Pompidou or turn your gaze inwards, to the café's chic clientele.

La Belle Hortense
31 rue Vieille-du-Temple, 4th [C2]
Tel: 01 48 04 71 60
This wine bar and bookshop is one of the few non-smoking bars in Paris.

Berthillon
31 rue St-Louis-en-L'Ile, 4th [B4] Tel: 01 43 54 31 61. The Xanadu of ice cream, Berthillon offers 70 fantastic flavours (closed July/August).

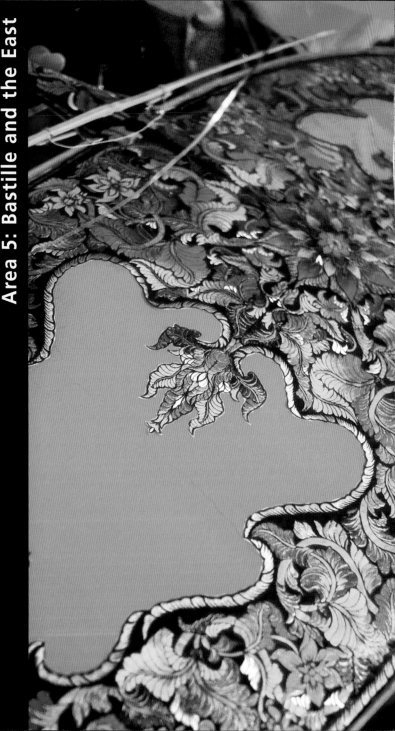

BASTILLE AND THE EAST

Explore the scruffy but vibrant working-class districts for off-beat boutiques, exotic food shops and cool cafés. Paris at its Bohemian best.

Traditionally the capital has been divided into north and south (or right and left) but these days the division between the east and west is more marked. The eastern, poorer side of Paris has long been associated with the workers and – unsurprisingly – social rebellion, beginning with that most famous revolutionary act of them all, the storming of the Bastille. This was the heartland of the Paris Commune, and today trade unions still begin their labour day marches at Bastille.

Opposite: Kites from La Maison du Cerf-Volant are brightly coloured and beautifully made.

Architecturally, the east of the city suffered under the reforming drive of the 1960s and '70s. However, it's the tantalising whiff of a less salubrious past, of a grittier, less-conventional lifestyle, that make the most appealing areas in the east – namely Oberkampf, République and Bastille – such refreshing alternatives to the bourgeois conservatism of the western *arrondissements*. The east is certainly very run down in parts, but where sophistication and glamour may be lacking, creativity and youthful energy abound. Shoppingwise, the east can't compete with the label-laden flashy boutiques that you will find in the west of the capital, but if you are on the lookout for something unusual that you would never come across in the more conventional stores, this is the place to come.

Around Bastille

First-time visitors should be warned that there is nothing to see in the way of a prison at Bastille. The old stronghold was entirely dismantled, and a bank now occupies its site. The column on the place de la Bastille is actually a memorial to lives lost in the 1830 and 1848 revolutions. The Opera house, on the other hand, can't be missed. One of Mitterrand's grand schemes, the Opera Bastille, completed in 1989, aimed to bring the traditionally elitist arts to the masses. Its popularist programme continues to earn critical disdain – not that it has had any impact on the opera house's great commercial success.

Our shopping tour begins on the rue du Faubourg St-Antoine, which runs from place de la Bastille down to Nation. From a shopping point of view only the first stretch of the street, as far as avenue Ledru-Rollin, is of interest, although *gourmands* may want to venture as far as the Marché d'Aligre (*see p118*) and the rustic Baron Rouge wine bar (1 rue Théophile-Roussel) for a glass of wine and plate of oysters.

The endless succession of furniture shops at the start of the street is in fact one company – Claude Dalle Romeo, gaudy purveyors of all things interior. It may not seem traditional, but this is a key to the Faubourg St-Antoine's past, when the area was packed with the workshops of furniture craftsmen. These days the furniture specialists are being squeezed out by Gap and its ilk, but there are still a few here and there, tucked away in the alleyways. For a flavour of the old place, take a detour down any of the passages you pass.

Equally gaudy but a rather less-likely fixture is Jean Paul Gaultier's shop, the one seriously famous designer in the area. Continue along Faubourg St-Antoine until you come to a turning on the left, rue de Charonne. The first part of this long road (as far as avenue Ledru-Rollin) and rue Keller,

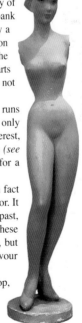

manage to maintain a villagey vibe – Greenwich, New York, rather than sleepy English that is. Look out for Isabel Marant, packed with sexy and stylish women's clothing, and the Pause Café, the perfect place to sit around looking quietly cool while you take a retail break. Nearby rue Keller looks pretty unprepossessing from the start, but along the left-hand side are several unique and delightful boutiques, mostly selling women's clothing.

Oberkampf and République

As a rule, Paris is a city that doesn't change that quickly, but recent history has proved Oberkampf the exception. This area just north of Bastille has come a long way since the slums of Edith Piaf's childhood. Even five or six years ago this was just another run-down district, but these days it is one of the hippest neighbourhoods in town. The vanguard may have moved on, but the bars, restaurants and clubs that make it so vibrant still remain.

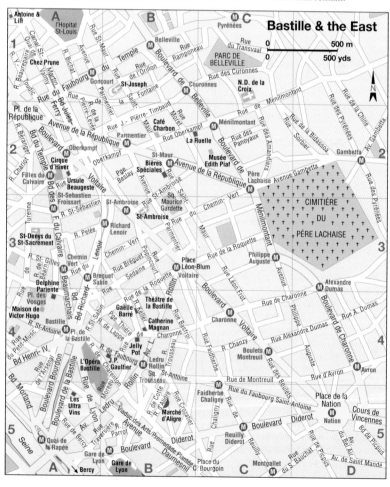

As for shops, Oberkampf is, admittedly, something of a lucky dip. You won't find any big names or chains here, but you will, if you're prepared to look, find that fantastically kitsch mobile-phone cover you've been looking for, or perhaps a rather 'unusual' skirt that you can be sure no-one back home will match. The shop might not be there the next time you come, but no doubt something equally intriguing will have taken its place.

Starting at the western end of rue Oberkampf the first shop of interest is Ursule Beaugeste at no. 15, one of the most fashionable and acclaimed hand-bag designers in the capital. The fun really begins, though, once you have crossed avenue de la République. This is the main strip, packed with bars, restaurants and unusual shops. Look out for trendy bars Le Mécano and Café Charbon. Two of the more interesting boutiques, on the other side of the street, are La Boule Magique, a magpie's hoard of jewellery and handbags, and, for front-line fashion, La Ruelle, a little further on.

If you are looking for some of the old flavour of the area, wander down the side streets off rue Oberkampf. Rue St-Maur, which crosses rue Oberkampf, and rue Jean-Pierre Timbaud are lined with tiny Middle Eastern food stores and cafés, retaining an aura of the area's Arabic inheritance.

Some of the city's hippest bars – and remember this is the east, so we're talking urban rather than glamour – can be found around the République area. Further evidence of impending gentrification can be seen around the Canal St-Martin, shielded by trees and dotted with small public squares and a popular spot for picnics and busking on summer evenings. Head for the bend in the canal, where you'll find the trendy Chez Prune and a row of pastel-coloured shopfronts belonging to Antoine et Lili *(see p70)*. On the opposite bank is the Hôtel du Nord, the subject and title of a 1930s French movie classic, and now host to occasional comedy nights in English.

Mitterrand's opera house looms large on place de la Bastille.

LOCAL ATTRACTIONS

The big tourist draw in the east is **Père Lachaise cemetery**. Laid out in 1804, it is here that you will find the final resting places of Héloïse and Abélard, Molière, Sarah Bernhardt, Oscar Wilde, Balzac, Proust, Colette, Edith Piaf and, most famously, Doors singer Jim Morrison, whose grave is now under police guard – someone has to fend off his over-zealous fans, even in death.

Many visit Paris without even registering the existence of the tranquil **Canal-St-Martin**, finished in 1825. The canal begins underground (supposedly to allow troops faster access to subdue potential uprisings), at Bastille, and surfaces to the east of place de la Republic, heading out of the city. With its nine locks it makes for an attractive boat trip (Paris Canal. Tel: 01 42 40 96 97).

Styles fit for a rock chick at Shine.

TIP
Don't miss your chance to join the mob dancing in the streets. On 13 July, the eve of Bastille Day, the firemen of Paris organise public balls across the city.

Fashion & Footwear

Anne Willi
13 rue Keller, 11th [B4]
Tel: 01 48 06 74 06
The look is a combination of the classic, clean-cut and feminine, with a slightly edgy eastern Parisian element. Clothes are tailored on the premises to ensure that perfect fit.

Antoine & Lili
95 quai de Valmy, 10th [A1]
Tel: 01 40 37 41 55
Yet another outlet for the hippy-chic purveyors. Their shocking-pink shopfronts have become a familiar sight all round Paris.
BRANCHES: across Paris

Catherine Magnan
39 rue de Charonne 12th [B4]
Tel: 01 43 55 56 57
Magnan's shops stock the designer's own creations. Sexy, slightly unusual women's clothes, with a strong emphasis on fake fur, and 1960s and '70s vintage.

Ekdotin
30 rue de Charonne, 11th [B4]
Tel: 01 43 14 06 39
Clothes here are brighter and bolder than you might expect – and with a distinct Tibetan influence. Perfect clothes for urban hippies of both sexes, with some accessories for your home to match.

Gaëlle Barré
17 rue Keller, 11th [B4]
Tel: 01 43 14 63 02
Gaëlle Barré specialises in fairy-tale women's tailoring: pretty clothes in an often unusual mixture of luxurious materials (mohair, felt, silk) and soft pastel colours.

Gravity zero
1 rue Keller, 11th [B4]
Tel: 01 43 57 97 62
Clubby clothes and accessories, for men and women, managing to mix the sporting and ethnic looks.

i-grek-bé
27 rue Keller, 11th [B4]
Tel: 01 49 23 51 13
She's a painter, he's an interior designer, and their boutique is a showcase for young designers of men's and women's clothing. The styles are paraded at the in-store *defilés* (fashion shows) they hold each month.

Isabel Marant
16 rue de Charonne 11th [B4]
Tel: 01 49 29 71 55
Beautifully designed but not (yet) at designer prices, Isabel Marant's clothes suit boho beauties who like their clothes effortlessly fashionable and discreetly sexy.

Jean Paul Gaultier
30 rue du Faubourg St-Antoine, 12th [B4] Tel: 01 44 68 84 84
As designers go, Monsieur Gaultier

is somewhat out on a limb setting up shop here – but then he never has been one to follow the mainstream. Outlandish tailoring for men and women.

Jelly Pot
30 rue de Charonne, 12th [B4]
Tel: 01 48 06 55 66
For sporting types and those who just like to look sporty. With an emphasis on all sports that involve a board, Jelly Pot offers clothes and equipment for both sexes.

La Ruelle
130 rue Oberkampf 11th [B2]
Tel: 01 48 06 71 50
The 1980s revival has made La Ruelle essential fashion shopping. For girls who like their clothes colourful and tight – where would we be without Lycra?

Shine
30 rue de Charonne, 11th [B4]
Tel: 01 48 05 80 10
If you've ever wanted to look like a rock star, Shine is a good place to start. There's something distinctly un-Parisian about the women's clothes here – probably because the owners have a marked preference for foreign designers, be they British or Brazilian.

Stella Cadente
93 quai de Valmy, 10th [A1]
Tel: 01 42 09 27 00
A light and airy boutique looking onto the Canal St-Martin with a lovely selection of feminine clothes – floaty floral dresses and skirts, soft woollens – and imaginative jewellery and accessories.

Jewellery/Accessories

La Boule Magique
98 rue Oberkampf, 11th [B2]
Tel: 01 43 14 25 75
An enticing collection of jewellery, bags and scarves from all over the world, catering for all tastes.

Jamin Puech
61 rue d'Hautville 10th [west of A1] Tel: 01 40 22 08 32
Baguette, tote, belt or clutch – if you're looking for a bag you'll find it here. There's something wonderfully indulgent and ever so slightly decadent about Jamin Puech's designs, which probably explains their popularity.

Ursule Beaugeste
15 rue Oberkampf 11th [A2]
Tel: 01 48 06 71 09
The brains behind Ursule Beaugeste, Anne Grand-Clément, started off designing shoes for Sonia Rykiel et al. These days she designs uniquely stylish bags, with very distinctive detailing.

Virginie Monroe
30bis rue de Charonne 11th [B4]
Tel: 01 43 38 52 18
Virginie designs her own jewellery and she likes it big, bold and colourful. She also sells a small selection of clothing from Paul et Joe and similar.

Did you know?
The best things in life are free: during October artists all over the Bastille and Ménilmontant area open their doors to all and sundry. Look out for Open Studios events.

Top: Clutch bag from Ursule Beaugeste.
Left: Jacket from Gaëlle Barré.

Treats for the kids at Apache.

Design & Interiors

Chimène
25 rue de Charonne, 11th [B4]
Tel: 01 43 55 55 00
Stocks a diverse range of ethnic gems, from pottery to throws.

Claude Dalle Romeo
2,10,12 and 14 rue de Faubourg St-Antoine, 12th [B4]
Tel: 01 44 75 71 99
Unashamedly, gloriously kitsch, this furniture empire is one of the last traditional traders operating on Faubourg St-Antoine. Even if leopardskin sofas are not your thing, it's well worth taking a look.

Books & Music

Bimbo Tower
5 passage St-Antoine, 11th [B4]
Tel: 01 49 29 76 71
This is one of the best (and only) places in Paris to find music that's off the mainstream beat. Particularly good for imports (especially Japanese), independent labels and underground sounds.

30 Fnac
4 place de la Bastille, 12th [A4]
Tel: 01 43 42 04 04
Fnac is a chain of stores that specialise in books, music and electronics. This store, however, is dedicated to music and DVDs only, offering an extensive selection, largely in CD format, from Piaf to Daft Punk.
BRANCHES: across Paris (*for flagship store, see p52*).

Children

Apache
84 rue du Faubourg St-Antoine, 12th [B4] Tel: 01 53 46 60 10
Bright, buzzy, and bursting with children's toys of all price ranges, there is everything here that a child could possibly wish for. There's also a cyber café.

Food & Drink

A la Petite Fabrique
12 rue St-Sabin, 11th [A4]
Tel: 01 48 05 82 05
Choose from some 40 different kinds of chocolate, from creamy *ganaches* and melt-in-the-mouth chocolate liqueurs to the humble bar. All made on the 'little factory' premises.

L'Autre Boulanger
43 rue de Montreuil, 11th [C4]
Tel: 01 43 72 86 04
Around 30 different kinds of organic breads from which to choose, all cooked in a wood-fire oven.

Bières Spéciales
77 rue St-Maur, 11th [B2]
Tel: 01 48 07 18 71
Beer, and plenty of it, from around the world – altogether some 17 nations are represented. More unusual brews come from China, Corsica and Poland, although there are plenty of the more familiar Belgian labels too.

Démoulin
6 bd Voltaire, 11th [A2]
Tel: 01 47 00 58 20

TIP
To get a feel for the east as it was, visit the massive market along boulevard Richard-Lenoir (weekend mornings only). It's huge and a great place to stock up on fresh fruit.

Démoulin's cakes and chocolates are irresistible. Their buttery *pains au chocolat* are famed.

Les Domaines qui Montent
136 bd Voltaire, 11th [B3]
Tel: 01 43 56 89 15
Few Parisian wine shops are prepared to feed you too, but at Les Domaines they offer breakfast and lunch. Wines are French, naturally.

L'Inconnue de la Bastille
Cour Damoye, 12 rue Deval/
12 place de la Bastille, 11th [A4]
Tel: 01 47 00 07 80
An unpredictable selection of wines in a converted cellar provided by Francis Gourdin, the man responsible for the produce of the Montmartre vineyard.

Les Ultra Vins
16 rue Lacuée, 12th [A5]
Tel: 01 43 64 85 81
Superlative collection of almost 2,000 wines, from the very cheap to the glass of a lifetime.

Specialist

La Maison du Cerf-Volant
7 rue de Prague, 12th [B5]
Tel: 01 44 68 00 75
Brightly coloured and beautifully made, the kites on offer range from the simple to the highly elaborate.

La Maison de la Fausse Fourrure
34 bd Beaumarchais, 11th [A4]
Tel: 01 43 55 24 21
From cushions to coats, both tasteful and tacky, the 'House of Fake Fur' allows you to indulge in all things strokeable and still be kind to animals.

Tonkam
29 rue Keller 12th [B4]
Tel: 01 47 00 78 38
This shop holds a comprehensive stock of comic-book or BD *(bande dessinée)* paraphernalia, but it specialises in 'Japanimation', making it a mecca for dedicated *manga* fans.

Did you know?
The storming of the Bastille was actually a bit of an anti-climax: the liberating mob only released seven prisoners.

WHERE TO UNWIND

Café Charbon
109 rue Oberkampf, 11th [B2] Tel: 01 43 57 55 13. The former coal shop is no longer as fashionable as it has been in recent years, but it's still very lively. Its lofty ceilings, ornate mirrors and red-leather sofas lend an air of dilapidated grandeur.

Chez Prune
71 quai de Valmy, 10th [A1] Tel: 01 42 41 30 47 A cornerstone of the newly trendy Canal St-Martin area. The perfect place to act out your beatnik fantasies – go in a black polo neck and don't forget to take a copy of Baudelaire.

China Club
50 rue de Charenton, 12th [B4] Tel: 01 43 43 82 20. The place to come if you're looking for a bit of old-fashioned glamour. The lights are permanently dimmed and the candles always burning – this is old-world sophistication at its

most seductive – added to which, the cocktail list is lengthy (makes the best Bloody Marys in Paris), and the Chinese food excellent.

Pause Café
41 rue de Charonne, 11th [B4] Tel: 01 48 06 80 33. The service is slow, and the setting is minimalist, but there are plenty of people to watch while you wait (who are there to be watched in the first place) and there's also a terrace for catching those rays. Sums up the tone of the whole area.

Le Train Bleu
Gare de Lyon, 12th [B5] Tel: 01 43 43 09 06 This may seem an unlikely recommendation, situated as it is within a busy mainline station, but it's worth seeking out. The belle-époque interior is one of the city's best examples of old-school elegance harking back to the golden age of travel.

Urban Regeneration

Head east to see a once derelict railway and riverport transformed by leading architects into two shiny new shop-filled attractions

T he area south of Bastille has become a potent symbol of urban regeneration in the 21st century. A disused railway viaduct and dilapidated wine warehouse district have been brought back to life, and are now thriving commercial and recreational centres.

Viaduc des Arts

Built in 1859, during the golden age of the railway, the Viaduc de Paris supported a railway from Bastille to Bois de Vincennes, at a time when the area between Gare de Lyon and Bastille was a thriving den of artisans. But, as the railways declined in the 20th century, the viaduct fell into disrepair. Thankfully, it was saved from demolition and reopened in 1998 as the Viaduc des Arts (15–121 avenue Daumesnil).

Designers at work under the arches.

Designed by architects Patrick Berger and Jamine Galiano, the project's aim was to provide a stimulating environment for local artisans and recognise the importance of local associations and traditions. It seems the architects have successfully fulfilled their brief.

The 50 or so arches beneath the viaduct have been converted into spacious glass-fronted *ateliers* (workshops) and craft boutiques. The diversity of creativity is impressive and from the street you can watch furniture makers, upholsterers, dress and jewellery designers, and painters at work. Not all of the space was given over to workshops – as well as the VIA gallery, a showcase for designers in the capital, the viaduct also houses the fashionable Viaduc Café (43 avenue Daumesnil, 12th, tel: 01 44 74 70 70), popular both for its brunch and late opening hours.

Promenade Plantée

Above the arches is the icing on the cake. The old railway tracks have been replaced by a leafy walkway known as the Promenade Plantée, providing a green breathing space among the urban regeneration. Stretching for some 4 km (2½ miles) along the viaduct and descending to ground level through the Jardin de Reuilly and the Jardin Charles Péguy – the Promenade is accessible via staircases from the street.

Wandering among the rose bushes today it's hard to imagine the thunder of steam trains chugging their way to the Bois de Vincennes. It's an excellent way to see the city from a completely different angle, and makes for a very pleasant walk in itself.

Bercy Village

According to a recent survey, 89 percent of Parisians are satisfied or even very satisfied with their neighbourhood. In Bercy Village, that figure leaps up to 96–99 per cent. This newly developed *quartier* in the south-eastern corner of Paris, is part of an ambitious programme for the redevelopment of the "New Left Bank". A driverless fully automated "Meteor" line – the first new metro line built since 1935 – now links Bercy to central Paris.

You may already have heard of Bercy because of the Palais Omnisports Paris-Bercy, a state-of-the-art stadium with a capacity for 17,000 spectators, which attracts big names such as Johnny Halliday (the Gallic equivalent of Mick Jagger, but you have to be French to get it). The more recent attraction is the neighbouring Cour St-Emilion, a trendy new shopping and entertainment quarter centred on the Place des Vins (Métro: Cour St-Emilion, Bercy). An official centre of commerce since Louis XIV's reign, the Cour St-Emilion was formerly a dock lined with stone-walled warehouses used for storing wine that was brought into the city via the canal. In recent years its brickwork has been given a good scrubbing down, and the warehouses converted into shops, restaurants and bars, with a multiscreen cinema complex. Purists may despair at the contrived nature of the whole 'village' but the result is a brisk trade in a previously overlooked area.

As you emerge from the metro station, the alleyway entrance to the Cour is more or less in front of you. Immediately to your left is the massive glass-walled bar/restaurant complex. This is Club Med World. The idea is that you enjoy a themed meal, and then book your holiday. Depressingly, this rather soulless and over-priced place is one of the most likely venues to find the locals. As you come out of the alleyway and turn right you'll find adventure outfitters Andaska and technical treasure house Komogo (no. 3–5). Right in front of you is Ciné Cité – this is Paris's biggest multiplex cinema, with 18 screens showing both mainstream and arthouse films, usually in their original language with French subtitles.

Turning back on yourself you will spot popular chains Nature et Découvertes, an eco-friendly store dedicated to the natural world, Sephora, which specialises in make-up and perfume, at no. 14, and next door, a branch of booksellers FNAC Junior. Further down, also on the right-hand side, you'll notice Animalis (no. 52–4), a huge store dedicated to providing everything you need for pampering your pets. At the end, Georges Truffaut is packed with plants and present fodder.

If the weather is fine, the cobbled courtyard has numerous bars and restaurants with outside tables to choose from. The food is unremarkable, but it's a pleasant place to rest and relax.

Below: Bercy Village, the new shopping and entertainment quarter.

SAINT-GERMAIN AND THE LATIN QUARTER

Literary tradition lives on in the bookshops, but chic boutiques dominate. Left Bank shoppers have Cartier more than Camus on their minds.

Paris once went by a golden rule: luxury on the right bank, literature on the left bank. Gradually, though, the sacred enclave of the intelligentsia has taken on a more materialistic hue as global fashion brands, well represented on the avenue Montaigne and rue du Faubourg St-Honoré, snap up prime sites in the 6th and 7th *arrondissements*. If Saint-Germain's literary credentials remain intact, it is thanks to Flammarion, Gallimard, Grasset and smaller publishers who have refused to be tempted by luxury groups' lucrative offers for their premises. As for the three monuments to the district's literary heyday, the Deux Magots, the Café de Flore and the Brasserie Lipp, they are certainly thriving even if most clients are more likely to be debating the latest fashions than existentialist theories.

Opposite: La Hune, the city's best-known bookshop. Below: Jewellery at Kathy Korvin.

The area takes its name from Saint Germain, cardinal of Paris in the 8th century. On his death he was buried in the 6th-century abbey of Ste-Croix-St-Vincent, whose name was then changed to Saint-Germain-des-Prés. The oldest church in Paris, it was a centre for Gallic erudition for centuries. Although little remains of its original details the church is still the heart of Saint-Germain, so it's the perfect starting point for exploring the area. The best plan is to begin with breakfast on the terrace of the Deux Magots café as the summer morning light fills the church's garden opposite.

Arts and minds

Heading east down the rue Jacob, filled with fascinating antiques and interior design shops, lies the elegant place de Furstemberg, which houses the Musée Delacroix – the artist moved here in 1857 when he began painting the murals in the St-Sulpice church close by. Further on is rue de Seine, the equivalent of London's Cork Street in terms of renowned art galleries. The adjoining rue Visconti and rue des Beaux-Arts are also prime artist territory. Moving east again, the rue Jacques Callot, rue Mazarine and rue Guénégaud are rich sources of African tribal art. Going south towards the boulevard Saint-Germain lies the rue de Buci with its fast-disappearing food market. Still, the atmosphere is as lively as ever, and there are plenty of cafés where you can catch your breath. Crossing over the boulevard Saint-Germain, make sure you check out rue de Tournon for its mix of high fashion, jewellery and design shops.

East of here, past the Palais du Luxembourg and its gardens, lies the frenetic place de Sorbonne. The university was founded in 1253 by Robert de Sorbon and has been the centre of the Latin Quarter's intellectual activity ever since. Not surprisingly, the area doesn't lack bargain bookshops, especially around the boulevard St-Michel and in the little streets near the ancient churches of St-Séverin and St-Julien-le-Pauvre north of boulevard Saint-Germain.

For food shopping, head east past Le Panthéon to the weekend market on rue Mouffetard. Originally the road to Rome, it is one of the oldest streets in Paris, though its appeal has been worn down by the hordes of tourists that tramp its cobbled stones. The place de la Contrescarpe, a favourite haunt of Ronsard and Rabelais in the early 16th century, still has a few attractive cafés around the Eglise St-Médard for people-watching.

Boutiques and antiques galore

If serious fashion shopping is more up your street, then backtrack down rue de Tournon and into the rue St-Sulpice. After taking in the works of Delacroix in the Eglise St-Sulpice and the lovely 19th-century square and fountain designed by Visconti, move west into designer kingdom. Streets to circle for true Parisian chic are rue du Dragon, rue du Pré-aux-Clercs, rue des Sts-Pères, rue du Cherche Midi (especially for those with a shoe fetish) and

LOCAL ATTRACTIONS

Le Carré Rive Gauche, with quai Voltaire, rue des Sts-Pères, rue de l'Université and rue du Bac as its boundaries, is a square kilometre on the Left Bank where a host of excellent antiques shops can be found. Every year from 29 May to 2 June the galleries display their most precious, original objects until late into the evening. **Le Panthéon** (place du Panthéon, 5th) is the resting place of the great and good of France. In September 2002 the remains of Alexandre Dumas, author of *The Three Musketeers*, were transferred here from his native Villers-Cotterêts. The inhabitants of the town were not amused by the abduction of their beloved author. Among the fascinating medieval treasures of the **Musée National du Moyen Age** (6 place Paul-Painlevé, 5th) is the tapestry cycle, *The Lady and the Unicorn*. The works, depicting allegories of the five senses, are displayed in a special circular room. The sensuous wood sculptures of the Russian-born Cubist sculptor Ossip Zadkine are displayed in the **Musée Zadkine** (100bis rue d'Assas, 6th). Major players in French literature, art, music and cinema are buried in the beautiful **Cimetière du Montparnasse** (3 bd Edgar-Quinet, 14th), including Jean-Paul Sartre and Simone de Beauvoir, Baudelaire, César Frank, Serge Gainsbourg, Jean Seberg and Zadkine.

rue de Grenelle. Cross boulevard Raspail to recover from your buying spree at the Musée Maillol (59 rue de Grenelle, 7th, tel: 01 42 22 59 58). The beautifully restored 18th-century Hôtel Bouchardon used to be the home of writer Alfred de Musset. Today it houses the voluptuous figures of sculptor Aristide Maillol (1861–1944). The café downstairs, with its vaulted ceiling, is a pleasant place to rest your limbs.

If you turn right from here down rue du Bac as far as rue de l'Université you hit the Carré Rive Gauche, a square kilometre embracing some of the finest antiques shops in the world. The most extravagant of these lie on the quai Voltaire, while the rue de Lille, rue de l'Université, rue de Beaune and the rue de Verneuil have the most refined treasures. Look out for the graffiti-covered home of the late singer/composer/rebel Serge Gainsbourg on the rue de Verneuil. His actress daughter Charlotte is hoping to turn the house into a museum in his memory.

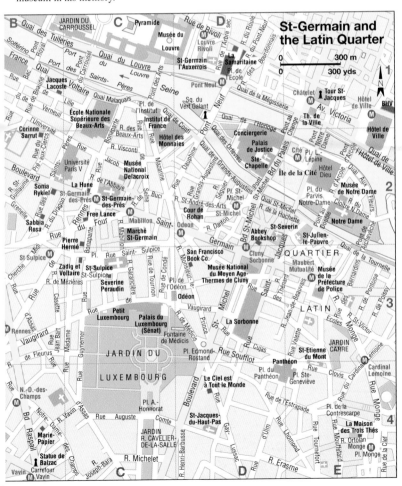

The 7th arrondissement

Past rue de Bellechasse, which crosses rue de l'Université, there is little shopping excitement until you reach rue de Bourgogne on the eastern edge of the 7th *arrondissement*. This elegant street leads into the cobbled place du Palais Bourbon, lying behind the l'Assemblée National, France's parliament. Trawl the street from the square southwards for its exclusive shops and galleries. Once at the top, you enter an area redolent of the French aristocracy of the 18th century, even though its superb buildings and courtyards are now France's political heartland.

At 77 rue de Varenne lies the Rodin Museum, housed in the lovely Hôtel Biron whose garden is the largest in the area after the Hôtel Matignon, the prime minister's residence at no. 57. It is worth synchronising your visit with the Journées du Patrimoine, or open-house days, to appreciate the interior sophistication of such residences as the Hôtel Boisgelin (the Italian Embassy) at no. 47 and the nearby Hôtel de Villeroy (Ministry of Agriculture).

Other streets oozing with cachet are rue Barbet de Jouy, rue Oudinot, mentioned in *Les Misérables* and home to Victor Hugo's father, and rue Monsieur, created in 1779 as an exit from the stables of Monsieur, the brother of Louis XVI, and later Louis XVIII. There is also rue Rousselet where writers Edmond de Goncourt and Barbey d'Aurevilly lived. This takes you into Montparnasse.

Montparnasse

In the 1920s and '30s artists and writers in need of some peace would descend on the cafés of Saint-Germain to escape the louche, carousing bars of Montparnasse where they lived and worked. Today the reverse is true. Famous haunts such as Le Sélect, Le Dôme and La Closerie des Lilas (where Hemingway spent his royalties) are tame, tourist curiosities. However, for a glimpse of the past, check out 126 boulevard du Montparnasse; go through the huge entrance to the end of the second courtyard where you'll discover a lovely house filled with artists' studios.

The streets of St-Germain are lined with chic boutiques.

Fashion & Footwear

Accessoire Diffusion
6 rue du Cherche Midi, 6th [B3]
Tel: 01 45 48 36 08
Accessoire designer Jean Paul
Barriol specialises in elegant soft
suede shoes that fit the feet like
gloves, yet are very hard-wearing.
BRANCHES: 8 rue du Jour, 1st;
36 rue Vieille du Temple, 4th;
11 rue du Pré aux Clercs, 7th.

Amin Kader
2 rue Guisarde, 6th [C2]
Tel: 01 43 26 27 37
Exacting designer Amin Kader
may not vary his designs much,
but this doesn't stop the steady
flow of regular clients to his tiny,
exquisite boutique. They just can't
get enough of his impeccably
finished classics, such as two-ply
cashmere pullovers, the jersey
cotton or silk tops and crêpe
de chine trousers and skirts.
His leather goods are so artfully
crafted they could be framed.

A.P.C.
3 and 4 rue de Fleurus, 6th [B3]
Tel: 01 42 22 12 77
Jean Toitou, the highly successful
proprietor/designer behind A.P.C.
assisted Agnès b for several years.
Yet his deadpan, DIY clothes have
more of a Muji feel, which is no
doubt why the label is a great success in Japan. The wacky accessories at No. 4 prove that Toitou
has a sense of humour.
BRANCH: 45 rue Madame, 6th.

Le Cachemirien
13 rue du Tournon, 6th [C3]
Tel: 01 43 29 93 82
Your appreciation of real cashmere will increase ten-fold on
entering this boutique. Italian
designer Rosenda Arcioni works
directly with Kashmiri artisans in
creating her aesthetic clothes that
blend tradition and modernity.

Feast your eyes and senses on the
embroidered shawls and scarves in
a delectable array of natural
shades.

Corinne Sarrut
4 rue du Pré aux Clercs, 7th
[B2] Tel: 01 42 61 71 60
Very Parisian fashion label.
Expect distinctly feminine 1940s-
style silhouettes in an original mix
of materials and colours.
Seductively simple wedding and
evening gowns are on show at
42 rue des Saints Pères, 7th.
BRANCHES: previous season,
24 rue du Champs de Mars, 7th;
7 rue Gustave Courbet, 16th.

Fabienne Villacrèces
18 rue du Pré aux Clercs, 7th
[B2] Tel: 01 45 49 24 84
Villacrèces opened her first boutique in St-Rémy-de-Provence
(she also has a branch in St-
Tropez), which perhaps explains
the radiant colours she uses for
her original, Midsummer Night's
Dream creations.

Free Lance
30 rue du Four, 6th [C2]
Tel: 01 45 48 14 78
Guy and Yvon Rautureau's shoes
are great to wear on bad hair
days – they are so wild that all
eyes will be fixed on your feet.
You might like to try the candy-
striped patent ankle boots,
the flower-covered pumps or the
Prince of Wales check stilettos.

*Top: Footwear
at Iris. Above:
Severine Peraudin,
specialist in stretch
eveningwear.*

*Supercool
Paul et Joe.*

BRANCHES: 22 rue Mondétour, 1st;
(men) 16 rue Bourg Tibourg, 4th;
22 rue de Sèvres, 7th.

Gelati

6 rue St-Sulpice, 6th [C3]
Tel: 01 43 25 67 44
Gelati keeps on its toes in following shoe trends, but its designs are
a third of the price of major fashion labels. Great colours too.

Honoré

38 rue Madame, 6th [C3]
Tel: 01 45 48 96 86
For mothers who like their daughters to be perfectly in sync with
their own style, Annick Lestrohan
and Stephanie Giribone offer mini
versions of their fresh-coloured
separates and eye-catching pumps.

Irié Wash

8 rue du Pré-aux-Clercs, 6th [B2]
Tel: 01 42 61 18 28
This Japanese designer offers
funky, daywear separates using
new materials he has concocted in
his workshop above. The Irié boutique next door houses his more
expensive, mainly evening wear.

Iris

28 rue de Grenelle, 7th [B2]
Tel: 01 42 22 89 81

Designers Marc Jacobs, Ernesto
Esposito, Alessandro Dell'Acqua
and Veronique Branquino rely on
Italian manufacturer Iris to produce their cutting-edge shoes.

Kristina Ti

50 rue des Saints-Pères, 7th [B2]
Tel: 01 45 48 62 35
This young Italian designer offers
a selection of gossamer-light
lingerie and swimwear. There are
also simple, practical separates
in natural fabrics, mostly silk
and cashmere.

Lagerfeld Gallery

40 rue de Seine, 6th [C2]
Tel: 01 55 42 75 51
This is designer Karl Lagerfeld's
style laboratory. Check out his
latest cuts or tour a photography
exhibition – very probably his own
work. Alternatively, just browse
through the latest fashion, beauty
and art press and the arty books
lying on the solid round table at
the gallery entrance.

Laurence Tavernier

7 rue du Pré aux Clercs, 7th
[B2] Tel: 01 49 27 03 95
You really need to be a lady of
leisure to do justice to Laurence

Tavernier's superb cotton or satin bathrobes and nightgowns. The alternative is to wear them out to dinner, but that could be risqué.
BRANCHES: 5 rue Cambon, 1st; 3 rue Benjamin Franklin, 16th; 32 rue du Bac, 7th.

Martine Sitbon
13 rue de Grenelle, 7th [B2]
Tel: 01 44 39 84 44
The scent of the designer's orange and mimosa candles draws you into this temple-like boutique. Beneath the vast ceiling, Sitbon's complex creations hang on stark railings like art installations. Among her wildly expensive accessories are dinky watches in aluminium cases on wide leather bands.

Mona
13 rue des Canettes, 6th [C2]
Tel: 01 43 26 10 37
Fashion editors know Mona so well the shoe boutique hasn't bothered to put its name on the façade. Designer names stocked here include Michael Kors, Marc Jacobs, Alberta Ferretti, Pierre Hardy and Alain Tondowski.

Nana Ki
5 rue de Condé, 6th [C3]
Tel: 01 55 42 95 26
Hidden in a back street, this tiny boutique is like buried treasure for BoBos (bourgeois bohemians). The designer uses Indian raw silk in scintillating colours to create pretty shirt-dresses, blouses, pedal pushers, bags and purses, some embroidered, some plain.

Ombeline
17 rue de Bourgogne, 7th [A1]
Tel: 01 47 05 56 78
Queen of kid shoes in the 1970s, Maud Frizon still has a celebrity clientele. However, the lady in question and her creations can be found exclusively at Ombeline. The 'Maud Frizon' boutiques are no longer her concern.

Onward
147 bd Saint-Germain, 6th [C2]
Tel: 01 55 42 77 56
Onward is an ever-evolving show-case for the most promising experimental young designers and established *enfants terribles*. The roll call might include Stolen Memories, Lutz, Preen and Markus Lurfer. Staples of the house are Dries Van Noten, Alexander McQueen, Yoshiki Hishinuma and Viktor & Rolf.

Paul et Joe
62 rue des Saint Pères, 7th [B2]
Tel: 01 42 22 47 01
The fetish boutique of Parisian fashionistas, it is filled with weathered looking creations that emulate the continuing vintage craze.
BRANCHES: 46 rue Etienne Marcel, 2nd; (men) 40 rue du Four, 6th.

Robert Clergerie
5 rue du Cherche Midi, 6th [B3]
Tel: 01 45 48 75 47
This shoesmith's inventive spirit rarely falters. It is no doubt this and the guaranteed comfort of

TIP

Parisians traditionally go shopping after lunch on Saturday, so if you prefer to browse in relative peace, shop in the morning.

Left: Belt from Paul et Joe.
Bottom: Bright BoBo design, Nana Ki.

Clergerie's creations that earned him his spurs as shoe designer for Yves Saint Laurent.

BRANCHES: 46 rue Croix des Petits Champs, 1st; 18 avenue Victor Hugo, 16th.

Sabbia Rosa

73 rue des Saints-Pères, 6th [B2]
Tel: 01 45 48 88 37

This is lingerie heaven. Relax on the leather sofa as Moana Moatti spreads before you satin, silk and chiffon negligees in delicious shades of tangerine, lemon, mocha and pistachio. The stock is in size medium, but all her designs, from silk bras and pants to flowing robes, can be made to measure.

Severine Peraudin

5 place St Sulpice, 6th [C3]
Tel: 01 43 54 23 16

This French designer works with superfine layers of stretch

Delicate layers by Severine Peraudin.

polyamide to create understated evening wear in two or three tones, such as turquoise and tangerine, or pistachio and terracotta.

Sonia Rykiel

175 bd Saint-Germain, 6th [B2]
Tel: 01 49 54 60 60

Sonia Rykiel caters for the modern woman – offering her witty, wearable and beautifully cut designs for work or play.

BRANCHES: (childrenswear) 4 rue de Grenelle, 6th; (sport) 6 rue de Grenelle, 6th; (men) 194 bd Saint-Germain, 7th; (women) 70 rue du Faubourg St-Honoré, 8th.

Stealth

42 rue du Dragon, 6th [B2]
Tel: 01 45 49 24 14

Marcus Klosseck, a New York-based record producer and designer, is the wit behind this hot boutique. His men's label Aem Kei (the phonetic rendering of his initials) blends New York street style with European chic. His women's line Aem Aya is equally sought-after. Other names to discover here are Tsumori Chisato, Fake of London, Haseltine and Poetry of Sex.

Tara Jarmon

18 rue du Jour, 6th [C2]
Tel: 01 46 33 26 60

Tara Jarmon's designs are modern yet timeless, feminine yet simple. She uses lots of fresh colours and natural fabrics in an Audrey Hepburn style.

BRANCHES: 73 av Champs-Elysées, 8th; 51 rue de Passy, 16th.

Vanessa Bruno

25 rue St-Sulpice, 6th [C3]
Tel: 01 43 54 41 04

Vanessa Bruno's individual clothes have a quiet femininity. Working-girl skirts and trousers with unusual cuts are matched with skinny tops and sweaters in a refreshing range of colours. Lots of embroidered handbags to set off the look.

Victoire Hommes
15 rue du Vieux Colombier, 6th
[B3] Tel: 01 45 44 28 02
Victoire will appeal to men not averse to a flash of colour. Her shirts come in lots of groovy shades and stripes, and some have Liberty patterns inside the cuffs. Solid classic shoes by Sam Walker Cheaney. Suave one-off scarves and hats and cute boxer shorts are among her dandy accessories.
BRANCHES: 10–12 rue du Colonel-Driant, 1st; 4 rue Duphot, 1st.

Yohji Yamamoto
3 rue de Grenelle, 7th [B2]
Tel: 01 42 84 28 87
Yohji Yamamoto's masterful cuts and finishes are on display in this museum-like space. As his work is mostly in black, it's a sober place in which to browse. However, when he does colour, expect a blast of brilliance.
BRANCHES: 47 rue Etienne Marcel, 1st; 25 rue du Louvre, 1st; 69 rue des Saints-Pères, 6th.

Zadig et Voltaire
1 rue du Vieux Colombier, 6th
[C3] Tel: 01 43 29 18 29
Trendy designs in leather, suede, nylon, velvet and flannel for men and women about town. A regular turnover of cutting-edge designers deposit work here, such as the blacker-than-black creations of Moon Young Hee. The sophisticated work of Jean Colonna comes and goes in stock.
BRANCHES: 9 rue du 29 Juillet, 1st; 4, 12 rue Ste-Croix de la Bretonnerie, 4th.

Jewellery/Accessories

Agnès b Voyage
15 rue du Cherche Midi, 6th
[B3] Tel: 01 45 44 44 63
In this cool, calm subsidiary of Agnès b clothes shops you'll find

Olfactory delights at Frédéric Malle (see p87).

elegant belts and watches, effortlessly chic bags, wallets and luggage, at surprisingly modest prices.
BRANCH: 10 rue du Jour, 1st.

Galerie Hélène Porée
1 rue de l'Odéon, 6th [C3]
Tel: 01 43 54 17 00
Around 40 international designers are represented in this minimalist jewellery gallery. Note the three-dimensional geometric pieces by Chavent, the beautiful delicate baubles of Alexandra Bahlmann, the necklaces comprised of tiny plaques of gold by Dorothée Striffler and the amazing paper cut-out effects by Nel Linssen.

Irina Volkonskii
45 rue Madame, 6th [C3]
Tel: 01 42 22 02 37
The muse of designer Jean-Charles de Castelbajac has set up shop selling her multi-coloured Plexiglas jewellery including handcuff bracelets, sushi still-life brooches and 'lit cigarette' pins. She also does vintage blouses jazzed up with her jewellery.

Joyce & Co
1 place Alphonse-Deville, 6th
[B3] Tel: 01 42 22 05 69
The woman who needs a bag for every occasion should check out this compact boutique. Super-glam day and evening creations with shoes and hats to match.

Did you know?

In 1997 a band of intellectuals formed SOS Saint-Germain to save the area's intellectual soul. They chose as its figurehead 1950s' celebrity Juliette Gréco, who sang in the infamous Tabu bar on rue Dauphine. As she no longer lives in Saint-Germain, credibility in the association is, however, wanting.

Right: Shu Uemura skin-wear. Far right: Glass jewellery and vigilant shop cat at Irina Volkonskii.

Did you know?

Oscar Wilde died 'beyond his means' at the newly renovated l'Hotel (13 rue des Beaux Arts). Worth a peek for its over-the-top decor by Jacques Garcia even if staying here is beyond your means too.

Just Campagne
159 bd Saint-Germain, 6th [C2]
Tel: 01 42 84 87 46
Leather-goods designer for the menswear chain Façonnable, Azzedine Berkouk is flexing his nimble, thimbled fingers with this luxury handbag boutique. His leather bags in vivid colour weaves are particularly fetching.

Kathy Korvin
13 rue du Tournon, 6th [C3]
Tel: 01 56 24 06 66
This Franco-American designer specialises in fairy light silver jewellery using semi-precious stones, feathers and Swarovksi crystals.

Kyo
32 rue du Dragon, 6th [B2]
Tel: 01 42 22 67 67
Sportswear watch collectors cannot fail to find a natty choice at Kyo, which imports all its models from Japan, including one-off and vintage designs. Among the hottest logos stocked are G-Shock, Nixon, Zucca, Adidas, Nike, Spoon and GSX.

Marie Mercie
23 rue St-Sulpice, 6th [C3]
Tel: 01 43 26 45 83
The more surreal the creations in this hat shop, the bigger the crowds. Step out in a black beret with a baby doll face painted on it, or wear a stiletto-heeled shoe on your head and save your feet. Hats made-to-measure take 10 days.

Naïla de Monbrison
6 rue de Bourgogne, 7th [A1]
Tel: 01 47 05 11 15
Some of the most exquisite and original jewellery in Paris lies in the dark-wood cabinets of this formidable gallery. You might find a silver necklace as solid as a breastplate, a cuff bracelet with topaz stuffed into layers of bronze or a ring made from a quail's egg.

La Reine Margot
7 quai de Conti, 6th [C1]
Tel: 01 43 26 62 50
Proprietor Gilles Cohen invites renowned international jewellers to create modern pieces using ancient stones, amulets, seals and scarabs tracked down by the gallery. The result is exquisite works of art at surprisingly affordable prices.

Health & Beauty

L'Artisan Parfumeur
24 bd Raspail, 7th [B2]
Tel: 01 42 22 23 32
L'Artisan Parfumeur has plenty of intriguing bouquets. For subtle punch try *Dzing!* or *Passage d'Enfer*. Vanilla addicts will appreciate *Mûres et Musc*, a bestseller here for over 20 years.

BRANCHES: 32 rue du Bourg-Tibourg, 4th; 22 rue Vignon, 9th.

Diptyche

34 bd Saint-Germain, 5th [E3]
Tel: 01 43 26 45 27

Although Diptyche's superb scented candles and eau de toilettes are increasingly available abroad, there is nothing like a visit to the three founders' glorious boutique. Close your eyes as you inhale a field of jasmine, mimosa, honeysuckle, broom or new-mown hay.

Editions de Parfums
Frédéric Malle

37 rue de Grenelle, 7th [B2]
Tel: 01 42 22 77 22

The grandson of Parfums Christian Dior's founder, Frédéric Malle, gave seven of the world's leading 'noses' carte blanche to create a fragrance under their own names. Judge the results for yourself in his elegant boutique.

Maître Parfumeur et Gantier

84bis rue de Grenelle, 7th [B2]
Tel: 01 45 44 61 57

In the 18th century there were 250 'parfumeurs et gantiers' in Paris, the salons where ladies went to have their gloves perfumed, buy powder for their hair and scent. Today, perfumer Jean Laporte keeps the spirit of the tradition alive with his cosy opera-box of a boutique. Besides nostalgic scents such as *Eau de Camellia*, *Laporte* is good at vegetables. His celery-based *Grain de Plaisir* eau de toilette is irresistible and the basil-based *Bai-Mé* is worth a try too.

BRANCH: 5 rue des Capucines, 1st.

Samuel Par

46 rue Madame, 6th [C3]
Tel: 01 45 49 22 21

The white-washed floorboards and therapeutic aromas at Samuel Par urge you to drop those urban defences and step out of your heels. Hot towels laid on the face or body are the first steps to relaxation. A facial Revitaliser made from Provençal plant extracts is almost as good as an airline ticket to Nice.

Shu Uemura

176 bd Saint-Germain, 6th [C2]
Tel: 01 45 48 02 55

The eminent Japanese make-up artist Shu Uemura learned his trade making up Hollywood movie stars of the 1950s, including Lauren Bacall, who still buys his best-selling cleansing lotion. Uemura began sharpening eyebrow pencils in Tinsel Town, which gave him the idea for the Hard Formula Pencil, his cult eyebrow liner. So hot is this gentleman today that L'Oréal recently bought a controlling stake in the company.

TIP

For the best sightseeing in between shopping in the 7th arrondissement, plan your visit around a Journée de la Patrimoine (open-house day), when the public has access to some of the most splendid 18th-century *hôtels particuliers*.

*Baby boutique,
Bon Ton (see p91).*

Department Stores

Le Bon Marché
24 rue de Sèvres, 7th [B3]
Tel: 01 44 39 80 00
Le Bon Marché is the slickest,
most user-friendly department
store in Paris. Highlights of the
fluidly designed ground floor are
the Theatre of Beauty, devoted to
the hottest make-up artist brands,
and the men's section Balthazar
with its polished wood floors and
designer boutiques. The first floor
has the cutest Parisian fashion
labels and international brands;
the third floor is for a sportier look
or, at the other extreme, lounge
lizards in search of sun wear.

Design & Interiors

Avant Scène
4 place de l'Odéon, 6th [C3]
Tel: 01 46 33 12 40
Minimalist decor is certainly
not for Elisabeth Delacarte, who
stocks elaborate contemporary
furniture and lighting of a baroque
persuasion. She favours European
designers such as Hervé Van der
Straeten, Franck Evennou and
Hubert le Gall.

Catherine Memmi
32–4 rue St-Sulpice, 6th [C3]
Tel: 01 44 07 22 28
At last the minimalist elegance
of Catherine Memmi has evolved:
three shades of green have been
added to her monochrome range of
exclusive bedlinen, tablecloths,
nightshirts, candles and exotic
wood furniture.

Dîners en Ville
27 rue de Varenne, 7th [B2]
Tel: 01 42 22 78 33
This tableware specialist stocks
Biot-made wine glasses and
tumblers in tantalising colours
such as tangerine, pistachio, lemon
and raspberry. They also stock
fancy tablecloths, silver cutlery and
Italian earthenware.

Mis en Demeure
*27 rue du Cherche Midi, 6th
[B3] Tel: 01 42 22 81 48*
If the scented candles of Diptyche
are a little out of your price range,
those by Mis en Demeure are a
good substitute – try the cinnamon,
grapefruit or orange. Upstairs the
interior design shop has chic
Provençal-style furnishings and
bed-linen, as well as inexpensive
paintings by little-known, but
talented artists.

Pierre Frey

1 and 2 rue de Furstemberg, 6th [C2] Tel: 01 46 33 73 00

Pierre Frey draws much of its inspiration from 18th- and 19th-century French fabrics, particularly the work of celebrated fabrics house Braquenié. As a compliment to these rich patterns, Frey also offers the luxuriant Thai silks and subtle African prints of legendary designer Jim Thompson.

BRANCH: 47 rue des Petits-Champs, 2nd.

Le Siècle

24 rue du Bac, 6th [B1] Tel: 01 47 04 48 03

The limited-edition dinner services are inspired by arts and crafts techniques of the past, with a modern twist. One of the shop's specialities is *découpage* – an 18th-century technique of applying cut-out engravings onto tableware. Their table linen using Elizabethan 'Black Work' embroidery is particularly impressive. Sharon Stone, Jack Nicolson and Isabel Adjani are among the celebrity clientele.

Verel de Belval

5 rue de Furstemberg, 6th [C2] Tel: 01 46 33 03 20

The four families of craftsmen behind this fabrics house are driven by a passion for carrying on Lyon's silk-weaving tradition. It is certainly difficult to resist the swathes of rich materials in this jewel of a boutique.

Yves Delorme

8 rue Vavin, 6th [C4] Tel: 01 44 07 23 14

Deliciously soft cotton sheets with lavish thread counts to cater to those with a bed linen fetish. The colours, around 25 in total, are in keeping with the understated chic of the brand, unlike the prices.

BRANCHES: 96 rue St-Dominique, 7th; 25 rue St-Sulpice, 6th.

Art & Antiques

Le Cygne Vert

41 rue de Verneuil, 7th [B1] Tel: 01 40 20 08 41

Olivier Dufay exhibits works by 1920s' and 1930s' French sculptors Despiau, Wlerick, Gimon, Drivier and Malfray. The reflective, mysterious mood of these busts and figurines is a far cry from the declamatory style of the 19th-century masters.

Galerie 13

13 rue Jacob, 6th [C2] Tel: 01 43 26 99 89

Martine Jeannin offers a charming collection of out-of-the-ordinary objets d'art, including beautifully sculpted chairs, bird cages, screens and lamps. She also specialises in antique board games.

Galerie Arigoni

14 rue de Beaune, 7th [B1] Tel: 01 42 60 50 99

A seductive den, filled with irresistible vintage clothes and jewellery. It's one of the best addresses in Paris for authentic vintage couture.

Galerie Blondeel-Deroyan

11 rue de Lille, 7th [B1] Tel: 01 49 27 96 22

Blondeel-Deroyan is the reference for sublime French carpets from the 15th to the 18th century.

Art from the North at the Nordisk Galleri (see p90).

HP Antiquités-Le Studio
1 rue Allent, 7th [B1]
Tel: 01 40 20 00 56
Don't miss this exclusive gallery hidden in a side street off the rue de Lille as you can count on Marc-Antoine Patissier's exquisite taste in 19th- and 20th-century furniture and *objets d'art*.

Jacques Lacoste
22 rue de Lille, 7th [B1]
Tel: 01 40 20 41 82
The grace of this collection of 1950s furnishings is likely to convert even the most strident critic of the period. The work of craftsman Jean Royère (1902–81) who had a fascination for circles, will particularly impress.

Nordisk Galleri
3 rue de Tournon, 6th [C3]
Tel: 01 43 54 29 39
You may be in Paris to appreciate French art, but this gallery and book-shop devoted to Scandinavian artists and writers is too rare a find to miss. The beautiful Ingrid Fersing Ferreira will guide you round impressive paintings by late 19th- and early 20th-century Northern European artists.

Books

Abbey Bookshop
29 rue de la Parchmenterie, 5th [D2] Tel: 01 46 33 16 24
Fans of Mavis Gallant, Margaret Atwood and other Canadian literary lights will appreciate the large stock of second-hand books by their compatriots here. It is a good source of reference books, too, and the service is amiable.

La Chambre Claire
14 rue St-Sulpice, 6th [C3]
Tel: 01 46 34 04 31
In this intimate, almost rustic-looking venue with its tiled floor and wooden spiral stairway, you may be surprised to find a comprehensive collection of the latest international photography books and magazines. Five exhibitions a year and the freedom to browse to your heart's content.

Gibert Joseph
26 and 30 bd St-Michel, 6th [D2] Tel: 01 44 41 88 88
A second home for Sorbonne students, they come here to buy and sell text and reference books. There is a small selection of books in English. Gibert also stocks stationery, office supplies and music in its sprawling buildings.

La Hune
170 bd Saint-Germain, 6th [C2]
Tel: 01 45 48 35 85
Sandwiched between Café de Flore and Les Deux Magots, this great bookshop is home-from-home for intellectuals dedicated to keeping up the area's literary pretensions. Downstairs you'll find a fine selection of French literature and theory; upstairs densely packed shelves of art, photography, interior design, graphic art and fashion tomes.

Librairie Gourmande
4 rue Dante, 5th [E3]
Tel: 01 43 54 37 27
Devoted to the culinary arts, this bookshop is abuzz all year round due to the fame of its proprietor Geneviève Baudon and her appetising collection.

Librairie 7L
7 rue de Lille, 7th [C1]
Tel: 01 42 92 03 58
Given the exemplary collection of decorative arts and photography books here, as well as the cutting edge magazines, it's not surprising to learn that Karl Lagerfeld, arbitrator of 21st-century taste, is behind 7L. Helpful laid-back staff.

La Maison Rustique
26 rue Jacob, 6th [C3]
Tel: 01 42 34 96 60

TIP
The green boxes along the Seine are part of the Parisian way of life. Never mind the lurid postcards and cheap paintings, home in on the ancient, cellophane-wrapped books.

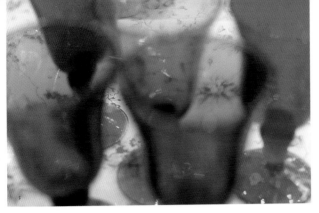

Gorgeous glassware at Florent Monestier (see p99).

Green-fingered consumers will fall for this bookshop packed with irresistibly illustrated oeuvres on the world's most sumptuous gardens. Plenty of practical gardening guides for those fluent in French.

Le Monde en Tique
6 rue Maitre-Albert, 5th [E3]
Tel: 01 55 42 73 73
Specialises in computer literature and stocks a vast selection of titles, including many in English.

San Francisco Book Co
17 rue Monsieur le Prince, 6th [D3] Tel: 01 43 29 15 70
Although the staff can be a bit gruff, this second-hand bookshop has an excellent eclectic range of English-language fiction. Flip through its stalls on the street for a good read for 1 euro.

Village Voice
6 rue Princesse, 6th [C2]
Tel: 01 46 33 36 47
Unbeatable for its selection of the latest English-language fiction, non-fiction, poetry and literary magazines. The staff is very helpful and the regular book readings unpretentious and efficiently run.

Children

Bill Tornade Enfants
32 rue du Four, 6th [C2]
Tel: 01 45 48 73 88

Bill Tornade's children's boutique is packed with cheeky, funky designs that are great for kids. The high prices, though, are strictly for rich adults.

Bon Ton
82 rue de Grenelle, 7th [A2]
Tel: 01 44 39 09 20
Choose from an eclectic mix of super-cool kiddie's fashion (age 0–10) colour-coded in trendy shades. Accessories include picnic boxes, hold-alls, boots and slippers.

Le Ciel est à Tout le Monde
10 rue Gay-Lussac, 5th [D4]
Tel: 01 46 33 21 50
Children and adults alike will have fun in this gift and toy store. Check out the PVC shopping bags with vivid floral patterns, wooden trains sets, colourful tents and kites, dinky gardening tool sets and adorable rag dolls.
BRANCHES: Carrousel du Louvre, 99 rue de Rivoli, 1st (for doll collectors); 7 avenue Trudaine, 9th.

Contre Vents et Marées
21 rue St-Sulpice, 6th [C3]
Tel: 01 46 34 03 27
A brilliant source of inexpensive practical clothes and seaside wear in natural fibres and pretty, muted tones for children up to age 10 and petite adults. Also does cotton sun hats and waterproof cloche hats.
BRANCH: 33 rue Vavin, 6th.

Browsing for a bargain at the San Francisco Book Co.

Petit Bateau
26 rue Vavin, 6th [B4]
Tel: 01 55 42 02 53
Children and women's underwear and sleepwear in the softest cotton and neatest shapes. Once you've worn a Petit Bateau cotton T-shirt, the prices of those flashy brand equivalents will seem ridiculous.
BRANCHES: across Paris.

Un Jour Un Jouet
8 rue de l'Abbé de l'Epée, 5th [D4] Tel: 01 43 2 97 01
This shop has a great array of toys (mostly wooden), including hand-crafted mobiles, puzzles and jack-in-the-boxes. Boutique Bass next door has fun objects and games for parents, so they don't feel left out.
BRANCH: 65 avenue de la Bourdonnais, 7th.

Food & Drink

Barthelemy
51 rue de Grenelle, 7th [B2]
Tel: 01 45 48 56 75
Follow the scent to this tiny cheese shop. Gems from around France are ripened to perfection in its cellars. Staff will take the time to explain the provenance and production process of their wares.

Debauve et Gallais
30 rue des Saints-Pères, 7th [B2]
Tel: 01 45 48 54 67
Messieurs Debauve and Gallais were chemists to Louis XVI, and their chocolates were considered good for the health as they had no added sugar – still the case today. The shop offers 40 varieties prepared in traditional copper vats and packed in royal blue and grey boxes that still look fit for a king.

Huilerie Artisanale
J Leblanc et Fils
6 rue Jacob, 6th [C2]
Tel: 01 46 34 61 55
Star chefs from around the world come to stock up at this tiny, unassuming shop. The Leblanc family produce pure oils from hazelnuts, almonds, pine nuts, peanuts, pistachios and, of course, olives.

La Maison des Trois Thés
33 rue Gracieuse, 5th [E4]
Tel: 01 43 36 93 84
Proprietor Yu Hua Tseng is one of the ten leading tea experts in the world. The blue-green tea dong ding wulong is among her specialities with a heady aroma of orchid, magnolia and blackcurrant. Experience gongfu cha, the ancient ritual of taking tea in Madame

Tseng's spacious salon. Be warned, though, tea is so sacred here that perfume wearers are not admitted.

Pierre Hermé

72 rue Bonaparte, 6th [C2]
Tel: 01 43 54 47 77
The rue Bonaparte was dead on Sundays before the arrival of *pâtissier* supremo and chocolate wizard Pierre Hermé. The queues for his aesthetic, architecturally constructed cakes are unending. As for the chocolates, their names – Balthazar, Intense, Sensations – do justice to their hedonistic impact.

Ryst Dupeyron

79 rue du Bac, 7th [B2]
Tel: 01 45 48 80 93
Treasures in this wines and spirits shop include around 200 premier cru Bordeaux, rare whiskies and vintage ports.

Specialist

Marie-Papier

26 rue Vavin, 6th [B4]
Tel: 01 43 26 46 44
Stocks hundreds of writing and artist papers from all over the world, including Japan, Nepal and Italy. A scribbler's paradise.

Sennelier

3 quai Voltaire, 7th [C1]
Tel: 01 42 60 72 15
Gustave Sennelier founded this aladdin's cave of artists' materials, in 1887. The shop conserves the ambience that delighted Kandinsky, Gauguin and Cézanne among others. Rare pigments derived from lapis lazuli and malachite, gold leaf and hundreds of delicious shades of oils, pastels and watercolours are among the treasures on offer.

WHERE TO UNWIND

Le Bar du Marché
75 rue de Seine, 6th [C2] Tel: 01 43 26 55 15
A lively spot facing the Buci market for a cheap and cheerful breakfast or aperitif.

La Coupole
102 bd du Montparnasse, 14th [B4]
Tel: 01 43 20 14 20. This vast, legendary restaurant is always making a comeback. Crowds of Parisians and tourists mingle good-naturedly on the banquettes. Expect to be adequately fed – not a gastronomic experience.

La Fourmi Aillée
8 rue du Fouarre, 5th [E2] Tel: 01 43 29 40 99
There's a Bloomsbury-set ambience in this tea salon with its high, book-lined walls, collection of blue and white teapots and cosy fireplace. It offers an original blend of fruit and Indian teas and excellent home-made tarts.

Institut du Monde Arabe
1 rue des Fossés-St-Bernard, 5th [east of E3]
Tel: 01 40 51 38 38. Admire the views from the lovely rooftop restaurant of this impressive modern institute incorporating exhibition and concert halls for Arab art and music. There's also a cool, laid-back café downstairs.

Luxembourg Palace and Gardens
Place Edmond-Rostand [D3] or rue Vaugirard, 6th [C3] Built in the 1620s for Marie de Médicis, widow of Henri IV, the palace resembles the Pitti Palace in her native Florence. The gardens, a mix of formal and 'English-style' have both intimate squares and open vistas.

La Palette
43 rue de Seine, 6th [C2] Tel: 01 43 26 68 15
A more sophisticated café for a light lunch or evening drink with a large terrace animated by local galley owners.

Le Rostand
6 place Edmond-Rostand, 6th [D3]
Tel: 01 43 54 61 58. This spacious café with mahogany bar and polished-brass fixtures is located opposite the Luxembourg gardens.

WEST OF INVALIDES

Saunter down the wide boulevards of the well-heeled west, lined with exclusive shops, galleries and 'traiteurs' filled with gourmet delights

The Eiffel Tower is ever-present west of Les Invalides. Stretching almost 320 metres high, its iron girders loom like the limbs of a giant playing hide and seek among the grand apartment blocks of the 7th *arrondissement*. Curiously, though, the six million-plus tourists who visit the monument every year hardly venture beyond the Champ de Mars. Indeed, the area remains one of the quietest districts in Paris. True, its spartan-looking avenues, all named after soldiers, can be a little off-putting for pleasure seekers – which perfectly suits the senior civil servants, captains of industry and rich, retired Americans who have sumptuous apartments here. Yet, uninspiring as it might at first appear, this area has pockets of charm, and some very special shops, that make the western 7th very rewarding to explore.

Opposite: Style from Lili la Tigresse, Passy. Below: Try Wu' Gallery for as-yet-unknown designers.

Les Invalides to rue Cler

The ideal place to start is the place des Invalides – the grass-covered parkland that splits the parallel streets of rue de Grenelle, rue Saint Dominique and rue de l'Université into east and west. It invariably smells of freshly cut grass and is a great place to relax after taking in the formidable art collection of the Musée d'Orsay on Quai Anatole France, a ten-minute walk to the east. The views from here on to the Hôtel des Invalides in one direction and the Alexander III bridge in the other are majestic indeed.

From here, you can take the rue de l'Université west, crossing over the plane-tree-lined boulevard de la Tour Maubourg where the exclusive caviar shop and restaurant Petrossian beckon you back into Russia's golden age. A little further on, rue Surcouf is the first of a cluster of small streets that retain an artisanal ambience, left over from when the area was an important craft centre in the 18th and 19th centuries. Nearby is rue Malar, dotted with *traiteurs* (upmarket French takeaways) offering homemade gastronomic delicacies.

Paradoxically, amidst this enclave of little streets still nurturing independent artisans is rue Cognacq-Jay, named after Ernest Cognacq, founder of one of Paris' oldest department stores, La Samaritaine, and his wife Louise Jay. (The museum of the same name, showcasing the couple's fine collection of French 18th-century art, is in the 3rd *arrondissement*; see p59)

Moving south, the early 19th-century church of St-Pierre-du-Gros-Caillou at 129 rue Saint Dominique is situated on the site of a famous boulder *(gros caillou)*, which gave the district its name in the 18th century. The rock marked the territory boundaries of the Saint-Germain des Prés and Ste-Geneviève churches who owned the land, previously known as the Grenelle plain, until the 17th century. It was thanks to the royal commissions to construct Les Invalides and later the Ecole Militaire that the Gros Caillou district grew and thrived.

Opposite the church is rue Cler and its tumultuous food market. This is one of the most convivial streets in the 7th, but make sure you come in the morning when the stallholders and store keepers are in full voice. At lunchtime local office workers head for the Café au Marché, a relaxed, typically Parisian bar/restaurant that is the antithesis of the stiff-collared 7th.

Strolling down the avenues

Once you hit the nearby avenue Bosquet, a chilly elegance prevails. However, it is this main artery and avenue de la Bourdonnais that offers the most interesting prospects for shoppers. Before entering the crowd-filled Champ de Mars, take time to savour the gracious, tree-lined residential streets west of the avenue de la Bourdonnais.

The Champs de Mars is a stretch of parkland that lies like a green carpet at the foot of the Eiffel Tower. This was the site of a market garden supplying vegetables to Parisians from the Middle Ages until the 18th century. After the Ecole Militaire was built in 1752 the 21-hectare (52 acre) area was turned into a military exercise ground with a capacity for 10,000 men.

Eiffel Tower to Village Suisse

The Eiffel Tower hovers above the Seine at the northern end of the Champs de Mars. Built for the Exposition Universelle in 1889, the tower was meant to be dismantled in 1909, but Parisians had grown used to the 'hollow candelabra', as the author Joris-Karl Huysmans disparagingly called it, and the

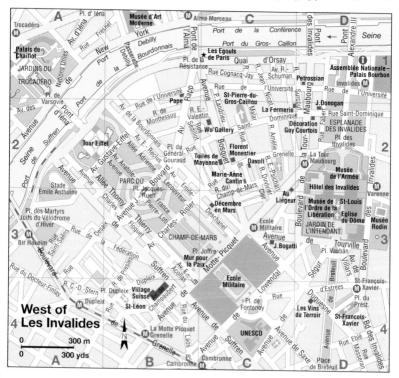

LOCAL ATTRACTIONS

From north to south: **Les Egouts de Paris** (entrance opposite 93 quai d'Orsay, by Pont d'Alma). The 75-minute tour of the Paris sewer is fascinating but not for those with a sensitive nose. Each sewer in the 2,100-km (1,300-mile) network is marked with a replica of the street sign above. The **Mur pour la Paix** – the 'wall of peace', a glass and stainless steel structure assembled in 2000 by star French architect Jean-Michel Wilmotte – stands defiantly opposite the Ecole Militaire on the place Joffre. The word peace is written in 32 languages and 14 alphabets on the wall. The **UNESCO** building (place de Fontenoy) would resemble a bunker if it wasn't partly constructed in glass. It's worth a visit, though, for the sculptures by Calder, Giacometti, Picasso and Arp, and the Japanese garden.

placing of a radio transmitter on top saved it from destruction. From the dusty place Joffre at the southern tip of the Champ de Mars there is an impressive view of the gardens and the Eiffel Tower looking like a soldier at ease against the skyline.

The Eiffel Tower looms behind every avenue.

Facing the tower, the Ecole Militaire is the work of celebrated 18th-century architect Jacques-Ange Gabriel. Louis XV commissioned the military college to help men of little means learn the art of soldiership. Bonaparte studied here for a year in 1784. He left as a sub-lieutenant with the recommendation: 'He will go far, circumstances permitting.'

To delve deep into the world of French art and antiques, head south to the Village Suisse at 38–78 avenue de Suffren. This area was actually a Swiss village, built for the 1900 Exposition Universelle. It was then transformed by modern apartment blocks, but the little squares beneath shelter around 150 antiques shops; place Genève and place de Lucerne are especially well-endowed with 18th- and 19th-century silverware, paintings and furnishings.

The Dôme

To return to the Hôtel des Invalides, the most direct route is via avenue de Lowendal or avenue de Ségur, but avenue de Breteuil is by far the prettiest. From place de Breteuil, the start of one of the city's loveliest markets (Thursday and Saturday), there is a stunning vista taking in the avenue of lime trees that leads up to the breathtaking, golden-roofed Eglise du Dôme, which houses Napoleon's tomb. The Dôme is situated at the southern end of the Hôtel des Invalides, commissioned by Louis XIV to house and care for retired soldiers. Today the hospital cares for around 100 men – in previous centuries it housed up to 7,000 ex-soldiers. Back on the pristine esplanade, stop to enjoy one of the airiest views found anywhere in Paris.

Fashion & Footwear

Chattanooga
53 and 71 avenue Bosquet, 7th [C3] Tel: 01 45 51 76 65
Stocks all the latest gear for skate-boarders, surfers and snowboard-ers. Casual clothes for off-duty sportsmen are available at the "downtown" shop at number 71.

Comptoirs Bourdonnais
45 av. de la Bourdonnais, 7th [B2] Tel: 01 47 05 70 63
An excellent source of second-hand, often hardly worn, hot fash-ion labels including Barbara Bui, Paule Ka, New York Industrie, Galliano, Prada and chic Paris labels. Prices are around 30 percent lower than the original mark up.
BRANCH: 2 rue du Regard, 6th

J. Donegan
38 rue Saint Dominique, 7th [D2] Tel: 01 45 51 69 15
Don't be thrown by the Irish name. This men's shoemaker is very Parisian, with 15 years' experience catering to the needs of well-heeled men-about-town. Its calf-skin loafers come in a variety of widths, and the range of glazes and patinas on offer is impressive.
BRANCHES: 18 rue Chauveau Lagarde, 8th; 103 rue de la Pompe, 16th; 128 bd de Courcelles, 17th.

Pape
4–4bis avenue Rapp, 7th [B1] Tel: 01 47 53 04 05
Senegalese tailor Ndiayéu Pape caters to international financiers and hot-shot businessmen. He will deck you out in a classically British custom-made three-piece suit with all the trimmings.
The shirts and accessories also have the unmistakable Pape stamp; there is even a Pape perfume.
BRANCH: 20 avenue George V, 8th

Stradel's
65 avenue Bosquet, 7th [C3] Tel: 01 45 55 91 29
This is a key address for dandies very particular about the cut of their cloth – Stradel suppliers include fabric kings Lora Piana and Cerruti. The boutique spe-cialises in narrow-fitting suits with the buttons placed high on single-breasted jackets. These have an outwardly classic look, but linings in mauve, green or deep pink give them a sartorial twist.

Jewellery

MZ Creations
10 rue Malar, 7th Tel: 01 45 55 77 26
Iranian jeweller Mina Zamani offers simple gold designs worked around precious or semi-precious

Florent Monestier, specialists in southern French style.

stones. Her tiny workshop attracts clients in search of custom-made pieces using stones they might bring themselves.

Health & Beauty

Claire-millia
40bis avenue Bosquet, 7th [C2] Tel: 01 44 18 34 34
Two beauticians, Claire and Millia, have created a cosy salon offering botanical face and body treatments, notably with Sisley products. Unwind with their hammam using soothing eucalyptus oil. They stock Wolford hosiery, too.

J. Bogatti
29 avenue de Tourville, 7th [C3] Tel: 01 47 05 00 31
Pampering starts at the entrance of this exclusive beauty salon with a uniformed doorman ushering you into the beechwood interior. Swiss-based La Prairie products are used for facials, but flagging shoppers should opt for the head-to-toe 'Soin Cashmere' – a hair treatment that uses essential citrus oils, followed by a shiatsu massage to the head and shoulders, a footbath and, finally, a massage with reflexology.

Design & Interiors

Au Liégeur
17 avenue de la Motte Picquet, 7th [C2] Tel: 01 47 05 53 10
A variety of household goods all made from cork, including wine stoppers, pitchers and tablemats.

Chisseaux Rive Gauche
33 av. de la Bourdonnais, 7th [B2] Tel: 01 45 55 49 17
Frédérique Forau is passionate about colour, and you will find lots of it in her very discerning gallery devoted to modern French

Left: Boards at Chattanooga. Below left: Cork homeware at Au Liégeur.

art. Her artist's register includes Robert Savary of the Ecole de Paris, Yvette Bonté from the Ecole de Provence and the figurative works of Michel Bezzina, who has a fetish for Venice. Forau named the gallery after Touraine's Château de Chisseaux, which she painstakingly restored.

Decoration Guy Courtois
69 rue Saint Dominique, 7th [D2] Tel: 01 47 05 26 52
Guy Courtois stocks lots of vibrant furnishing fabrics in quality cottons. Look out for the unusual fishing-boats prints and the fabrics with colourful African scenes that have canvas bags and purses to match. Closed Saturdays.

Florent Monestier
47bis avenue Bosquet, 7th [C2] Tel: 01 45 55 03 01
Florent Monestier has created a sunny interior-design shop that specialises in Provençal tableware, ceramics and furnishings, as well as pretty, traditional quilts from the Midi.

Did you know?
The Eiffel Tower weighs 10,100 tons in total, 60 tons of which are paint. The monument is re-painted every seven years, and the work takes 15–16 months.

*Bonbon Plume
baby boutique.*

Galerie Michel Gillet
*54 av de la Bourdonnais, 7th
[B2] Tel: 01 47 53 72 73*
Michel Gillet is a champion of popular art, exhibiting the best. Among the artists he represents look out for Fred Perimon's wild sculptures, Mathias Robert's 3D, cardboard paintings and the wry, primitive art of William Wilson. The gallery holds shows five or six times a year, including one themed show.

La Palférine
*43 avenue Bosquet, 7th [C2]
Tel: 01 45 56 93 81*
Strange but often beautifully executed paintings, furniture and decorative works fill this dimly lit, mysterious antique shop. Don't be surprised to find a large bulldog in papier-mâché eyeing you from his wicker chair, plates sculpted with huge artichokes or the portrait of a lady painted in double. Edgar Allen Poe material.

Techniques et Décors
*42 av. de la Bourdonnais, 7th
[B2] Tel: 01 44 18 36 96*
Exquisite hand-made wallpapers of grasscloth, sisal, bamboo and straw are available here, imported by Techniques et Décors from Korea and China. The Japanese have used such papers to decorate their temples for centuries. There are also household silks and taffetas by Lyonnaise silk weavers at very competitive prices.

Toiles de Mayenne
*36 avenue Bosquet, 7th [C2]
Tel: 01 45 55 40 50*
Toiles de Mayenne have been producing cotton furnishing fabrics since 1806 and their designs still draw on traditional patterns, including the graceful blue and white toile de Jouy. The boutique also stocks pretty, fabric-covered sewing boxes, photo albums and address books.
BRANCH: 9 rue Mézières, 6th

Wu' Gallery
*14bis avenue Bosquet, 7th [C2]
Tel: 01 47 05 45 38*
Designer couple Mas'oud Nasri and Marine de Wulf opened this pioneering gallery in 2000 to promote unknown, talented young furniture designers. Around 25 pieces are created a year in limited editions of around ten units. Among their success stories is Jean-Marc Gady who was recruited by Louis Vuitton following exposure at Wu'. Cutting-edge aficionados step this way.

Children

Benny Bunny
*64 av. de la Bourdonnais, 7th
[C3] Tel: 01 44 18 93 83*
Benny Bunny is a mine of designer clothes for children up to six years old at slightly cheaper prices than in the brands' own stores. Labels include Cacharel, Charabia, La Petite Ourse and Petit Faune.

Bonbon Plume
*22 av. de la Bourdonnais, 7th
[B2] Tel: 01 40 62 91 64*

This tiny space has everything a pampered baby needs for sweet dreams: a wooden cot, pristine sheets, quilts and pillows, dinky nightgowns, knitted slippers and cuddly toys.

Décembre en Mars
65 av, de la Bourdonnais, 7th [C3] Tel: 01 45 51 15 45
Décembre en Mars stocks a rare collection of artisanal toys, including wooden sailing boats, farmhouses complete with farming tools and kitchens with miniature stoves and tableware. Impeccably turned out disguises are also available, including knights of the Round Table, witches and warlocks. The wooden swords and armour made from silver cardboard are also expertly crafted. A delight for adults and children alike.

Food & Drink

L'Ambassade du Sud Ouest
46 av. de la Bourdonnais, 7th [B2] Tel: 01 45 55 59 59
Chef Aimé Lalanne runs both the restaurant and fine foods store at this address. You will find tins and jars of Basque piperade, coq au vin, cassoulet, confit de canard and a wide assortment of foie gras. In fact, the whole panoply of gastronomic triumphs of southwest France will be at your fingertips here.

Davoli – La Maison du Jambon
34 rue Cler, 7th [C2] Tel: 01 45 51 23 41
The Davoli family are Parma ham specialists, which is only natural as they come from the town. Davoli also stocks fine French and Spanish hams, including jambon de Bayonne. Its parmesan cheese is excellent, too.

La Fermerie
24 rue Surcouf, 7th [C2] Tel: 01 45 55 23 03
At La Fermerie you can try out succulent French regional dishes on the spot, then take them off the shelves for home consumption. La Fermerie's jarred marvels include traditional lamb stew, rabbit with summer vegetables and goose and duck cassoulets, as well as 100 percent pure quince, pear and raspberry juices.

Le Lutin Gourmand
47 rue Cler, 7th [C2] Tel: 01 45 55 29 74
For over 60 years the Lutin Gourmand has been churning out an irresistible array of very fine chocolates from its spot in the heart of the rue Cler market. The ladies here also offer around 100 different types of tea, blended on the premises.

Les Vins du Terroir
34 avenue Duquesne, 7th [D4] Tel: 01 40 61 91 87
Alexandre Gerbe is an exacting wine merchant specialising in

TIP
Every Thursday and Saturday, the gracious tree-lined avenue de Saxe, plays host to the Saxe-Breteuil market. The produce sold by the fruit and vegetable vendors, the charcuterie and cheese specialists, the fishmongers and olive sellers is as fresh as the rich residents expect.

Handmade wallpaper from Techniques et Decors.

Ham from Davoli, cheese from Marie-Anne Cantin and wine from Millésime.

privately owned vineyards. He is a member of the Federation Nationale des Cavistes Independents, meaning he picks his wines personally from the domaines. Gerbe holds wine-tasting classes once a month for up to 15 people.

Marie-Anne Cantin
12 rue du Champs-de-Mars, 7th [C2] Tel: 01 45 50 43 94
This shop's eponymous owner is renowned as a passionate defender of 'real' cheese, meaning unpasteurised, and the smellier the better. Tuck into her guide book to 150 different French varieties and you will appreciate her stance. Or simply taste her creamy St Marcellin, lovingly matured *chèvres* (goat's cheese) or nutty Beaufort.

Michel Chaudon
149 rue de l'Université, 7th [C1] Tel: 01 47 53 74 40
Previously with Maison du Chocolat and LeNôtre, the cacao-fingered Michel Chaudun set up his artisanal shop over 16 years ago. Regulars come for his truffles shaped like mini plaques (Pavé de l'Univeristé) and his famous dark chocolate discs made with tonka beans (Eclats de Fèves), but the real marvels are his sculptures, particularly the Tutankhamun

heads in white chocolate and the superb African tribesmen in dusky dark chocolate.

Millésime
27 avenue Rapp, 7th [B2] Tel: 01 47 05 67 79
At Millésime, sommelier Hélène Claus has created an intimate 'wine library' in which to present her superior selection of approximately 80 French wines. She is also building up a discerning choice of New World wines. Given a day or two's notice, she can organise an evening wine-tasting session for groups of up to eight people.

Noé L'Antiquaire du Vin
12 rue Surcouf, 7th [D1] Tel: 01 47 05 01 02
Rolando Marzari and Frédéric Beal are the pragmatic wine and spirits experts behind this tiny shop buying and selling rare elixirs. Their oldest bottles date back more than 100 years, including vieux millésime Petrus and Château d'Yquem.

Petrossian
18 boulevard de la Tour Maubourg, 7th [D1] Tel: 01 44 11 32 22
Petrossian's haughty blue-green façade is unmissable on this grand boulevard. Even if you can live

without Beluga caviar, the store is worth visiting for its old-world charm dispensed by the white-coated shop assistants. Besides the little black eggs, there is excellent Norwegian smoked salmon and, of course, authentic, 100-percent-proof vodka.

Sport & Leisure

Bosquet Golf
47 avenue Bosquet, 7th [C2]
Tel: 01 45 55 03 33
Korean couple Yong and Jinhee Doh appear to have cornered Paris' golfing market. Whether obliging shoemaker John Lobb or Hermès by supplying clubs for promotional events, or renting the exclusive Honma brand to visiting dignitaries such as Bill Clinton, they are on a roll. Cheaper golf club brands are also available for sale or rent, as well as golfing clothes and shoes.

Des Poissons Si Grands (DPSG)
45 boulevard de la Tour Maubourg, 7th [D2]
Tel: 01 47 53 96 95
If you're looking to catch a big fish, this is the place to come. Every imaginable fishing rod, tackle and fly is at your disposal, along with wading gear and all kinds of fish containers. They also have a mail order service.
BRANCH: 160 rue de Grenelle, 7th.

L'Esprit du Sud Ouest
108 rue Saint Dominique, 7th [C2] Tel: 01 45 55 29 06
As its name implies L'Esprit du Sud Ouest is devoted to everything to do with the south west, in a nut-shell: food and rugby. There are the rugby shirts of France's champions Biarritz Olympique, as well as those of major overseas teams. The gear is displayed behind piles of foie gras, confit de canard and bottles of Bordeaux. Just remember, play before you eat.

Did you know?
Some 12kg of gold leaf was required for the Eglise St-Louis at Les Invalides when it was redecorated for the 1989 bicentenary of the revolution.

WHERE TO UNWIND

L'Affriolé
17 rue Malar, 7th [C1] Tel: 01 44 18 31 33
The market menu here offers inventive dishes lovingly prepared by veteran chef Thierry Vérola. Prices are fair, and the tasty appetisers are a sign of the good things to come.

Le Café du Marche
38 rue Cler, 7th [C2] Tel: 01 47 05 51 27
Sit on the terrace with a coffee or a glass of wine and enjoy the best view of the colourful market. Hearty, traditional dishes.

L'Esplanade
52 rue Fabert, 7th [D2] Tel: 01 47 05 38 80
This restaurant has it all: breathtaking views of Les Invalides; floodlights; opulent decor by Jacques Garcia; a fashionable crowd; and good contemporary food. It's pricey, but you can just come for a drink or a snack.

Fontaine de Mars
129 rue St-Dominique, 7th [C2] Tel: 01 47 05 46 44. Situated in a dinky arcaded square next to a handsome 19th-century fountain, this restaurant serves French classics pre-pared by the friendly Boudon family.

Green Spaces
There are a few expanses of lawn in the area (place des Invalides, Champ de Mars, avenue Breteuil) where you can stretch out. Make the most of these – elsewhere in Paris even walking on the grass is usually forbidden.

Pegoty's
79 avenue Bosquet, 7th [C3] Tel: 01 45 55 84 50. An intimate, stone-walled tea salon that sets itself up as typically English, but the teas and cakes are far more exotic. A good pit stop for shoppers.

Exploring the 16th

Don't get stuck on the Champs-Elysées – there are upmarket shops in Passy, historic sites in Auteuil and greenery at the Bois de Boulogne

I n the western extremity of Paris, on the right bank of the Seine, sits the 16th *arrondissement*. The area constitutes a sizeable slice of the city – it's bordered by the Bois de Boulogne on the west, the Seine on the east, avenue de la Grande Armée leading to the Champs-Elysées in the north, and suburban Paris to the south. Not for those in search of the arcane or the avant-garde, this is the city's bastion of BCBG *(bon chic bon genre)*, full of smart residences inhabited by entrepreneurs, socialites, politicians and wealthy expatriates. The 16th is a never-never land of big hair, Burberry plaid, diamond rings, macaroons and Berthillon ice-cream. The reason most tourists and Parisians venture here is to visit one of the museums around the place du Trocadéro, or to gaze at the magical views to be had across the Seine to the Eiffel Tower.

Passy and Auteuil

In the southern half of the 16th lie the *quartiers* of Passy and Auteuil, 17th-century spa towns where the rich came to take cures for ailments of the age. Passy (Métro La Muette or Passy) has retained a villagey air, complete with cobblestone streets and staircases. One of the main shopping areas in the 16th is centred on rue de Passy. It is a bit of a hodgepodge but makes for a comprehensive consumer experience: cheap and chic chain stores such as Kookai and Morgan rub shoulders with prestigious international labels such as Guerlain, Kenzo and MaxMara. There are several ambassadors from trendier parts of Paris – Antoine et Lili, Tara Jarmon and Victoire among them – and a few shops of real originality.

Neighbouring Auteuil (Métro Eglise d'Auteuil/Porte d'Auteuil) is more pastoral. Considerably less commercial than Passy, the shopping here is sparse and, frankly, unexciting. But Auteuil is of significant historical and architectural interest. During the Revolution noblemen would hide out here disguised as staff or patients of the spa. Try to get within gawking distance of some of its magnificent 'villas' – groupings of cottages and gardens divided up from grander properties, often protected from bypassers' gazes by wrought-iron gates or, more disagreeably, scowling security guards. The best known are probably the Villa Montmorency and the Villa Boileau.

Bois de Boulogne and the Avenues

To the west of Auteuil lies the Bois de Boulogne, 9 sq km (3½ sq miles) of what was once a royal hunting reserve, today complete with landscaped grottoes, a boating lake, the Bagatelle rose garden, a children's amusement park, restaurant, Longchamp and Auteuil racecourses, a theatre and more. Avoid it at night, when less salubrious activities take centre-stage.

But don't let all this distract you from your true reason for being here. There is a second shopping area of note in the northern half of the 16th, concentrated along the avenue Victor Hugo, rue de Longchamp and avenue Raymond Poincaré (Métro Victor-Hugo). In the same vicinity, rue de la Pompe – where the second-hand outfit Réciproque has colonised a dozen or so shops – merits a visit if you are a designer-label junkie.

PASSY DIRECTORY

• **Anne Fontaine**, 22 rue de Passy. Superbly made white shirts in all styles from crisp simple cotton cuts, to ruffles and lace.

• **Bathroom Graffiti**, 98 rue de Longchamp. Everything – from soap to slippers to shower curtains – is imaginative and humorous.

• **Bonpoint**, 64 av Raymond-Poincaré. Good-quality children's clothes in adorable designs that are anything but stuffy.

• **Brûlerie des Ternes**, 28 rue de l'Annonciation. Wooden barrels bursting with coffee beans and tea leaves from every plantation in the world fill this shop and then spill out on to the street.

• **L'Entrepôt**, 50 rue de Passy. Furnishings, tableware, curtains and lamps in an eclectic mix of style and materials.

• **Franck et Fils**, 80 rue de Passy. Exudes luxury and elegance with a judicious mix of upmarket labels. Sumptuous lingerie and great hair ornaments.

• **Gioia**, 16 rue Jean Bologne. Bijou boutique selling exclusive costume jewellery pieces from various designers, often using semi-precious stones.

• **L'Hôtel Particulier de la Tour**, 4 rue de la Tour. An arbitrary assortment of Venetian glass, crystal vases, lampshades, candelabra, etc. Good for gifts.

• **Lili la Tigresse**, 9 rue Gustave Courbet. Lili's 'Deliciouswear' is full of frills, sequins and sorbet colours. Great fun.

• **Réciproque**, 88, 89, 92, 95, 97, 101, 123 rue de la Pompe. For the past 25 years, dowagers of the 16th have been bringing their couture cast-offs to this colony of juxtaposed shops housing clothes, furs, jewellery and hats.

• **Senso Più**, 71 avenue Raymond-Poincaré. 'Gallery of wellbeing' run by a team of experts including acupuncturist, aesthetician, practitioner of Chinese medicine, osteopath, masseur and make-up artist.

• **Why Not?** 108 rue de Longchamp. Racks of leather, furs and ruffles.

• **Women's Secret**, 56 rue de Passy. Simple, sporty clothes, lingerie, swimwear and cosmetics at lowish prices.

Below left: Bench, Balzac's house. Below: Venture off the beaten track.

MONTMARTRE AND PIGALLE

Beyond the tourist enclave, the narrow streets are dotted with quirky boutiques and local shops – not a chainstore or designer name in sight

Sitting atop its hill overlooking the rest of Paris, Montmartre has always stood slightly apart from the rest of the city. Legend has it that in AD 287, the Romans decapitated St Denis, first bishop of Paris, on the site of the Chapelle du Martyr (11 rue Yvonne Le Tac). St Denis calmly picked up his head and carried it to where the basilica of St Denis now stands. The village of Montmartre – or 'martyr's mount' – wasn't incorporated into the city boundaries until 1860. Today its most readily visible symbol is the white dome of Sacré Cœur basilica, begun after France's defeat in the Franco-Prussian War in 1870 and completed in 1914. In 1871, Montmartre saw the start of the Paris Commune, when the Montmartrois, led by Louise Michel, stood up to the right-wing government of Adolphe Thiers. At the top of the hill, Place du Tertre abounds in tourist bistros, gift shops and would-be artists, but once off the main tourist drag it is still full of incredibly picturesque narrow villagey streets, ivy-clad cottages and cobbled squares.

At the end of the 19th century, artists including Toulouse-Lautrec began settling the hill and depicting its bars and cabarets; Suzanne Valadon – and later her son Utrillo – had her studio in the entrance lodge of what is now the Musée du Vieux Montmartre; while in the early 20th-century, Montmartre saw the birth of Cubism, when Picasso painted *Les Demoiselles d'Avignon* in his studio in the Bateau Lavoir. By the 1920s, most of the artists had moved across the river to Montparnasse where rents were lower, but numerous studio buildings remain, some of them still occupied by artists.

Opposite: Archetypal French café that inspired the film 'Amélie'.

Below: Vin rouge, Cave des Abbesses.

Shopping in Montmartre

Shopping in Montmartre lives up to the area. There are few chainstores or the famous designer names found elsewhere, rather, original outlets with a distinctly bohemian edge, spreading out from place des Abbesses (where Métro Abbesses is one of only two in the city to still have its Art Nouveau glass canopy). Rue des Abbesses itself is the focus of Montmartre life, with the café Le Sancerre and Le Chinon, groceries and wine merchants amid fashion outlets such as streetwise Bonnie Cox and eccentric hatmaker Têtes en l'Air, running into rue Lepic with its food shops in one direction and budget bistros and bars up towards the butte.

Wander along the streets around Abbesses – rue de la Vieuville, rue Yvonne-le-Tac, rue des Trois-Frères, rue Houdon, rue des Martyrs – and you'll find *atelier*-boutiques by creative young designers who make their wares on the premises, emporia full of floaty skirts and neo-hippy flounces, offbeat second-hand shops, small specialist bookshops, craftsmen and little galleries supporting local artists. Hybrid rue des Martyrs could only exist in Montmartre – arty clothes on one hand, transvestites and the drag cabaret Chez Michou on the other. The Abbesses end of rue d'Orsel follows the trend for craft and design shops, but heading east from shady square Charles

LOCAL ATTRACTIONS

The sugar white dome of **Sacré Cœur** is visible from much of Paris, but as well as the views it offers from the top, is worth the visit for its over-the-top neo-Byzantine interior. For a taste of the area's artistic past visit the **Musée du Vieux Montmartre** or pay tribute to Truffaut, Guitry, Dumas fils, Dalida, Berlioz, Degas and more in the shady groves of the **Cimitière de Montmartre**. Across the boulevards in the 9th *arrondissement* are the **Musée de la Vie Romantique**, devoted to writer George Sand, and the **Musée Gustave Moreau**, which contains hundreds of the artist's symbolist paintings in an extraordinary double-height studio. Pigalle is the only possible home of the **Musée de l'Erotisme**, a collection of erotic art from every continent, while the feather-clad, cancan girls at the tourist-oriented **Moulin Rouge** and the more alternative charms of drag revues **Chez Michou** and **Madame Arthur** keep the cabaret tradition alive.

Dullin, its eastern half runs into the fabric emporia that surround the old St-Pierre covered market, laden with rolls of dressmaking and furnishing fabrics, raw silks and lacy voiles. Down the northern side of the butte, past the vineyard on rue des Saules (planted in memory of the area's winemaking past) towards the Mairie du XVIIIe is a busy residential area. The shopping hub here is rue du Poteau where you'll find several good food shops including the excellent Fromagerie de Montmartre and Greek, Auvergnat and Italian delis.

Goutte d'Or

East of Montmartre, around boulevard Barbès, the Goutte d'Or reflects the largely African and Arab populations of the area. Long run down, with a heavy police presence and a dodgy reputation, particularly at night, the area has undergone something of a change recently, with a conscious effort at slum clearance, rebuilding

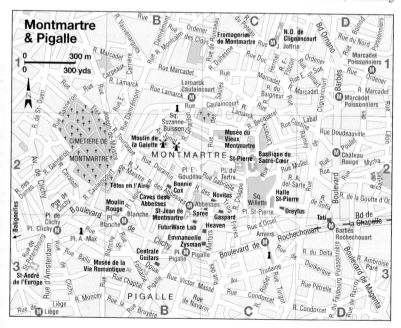

and tidying up, as well as projects such as the 'rue de la Mode' to encourage fashion designers to settle in the area. The twice-weekly market (Wednesday and Saturday) held under the Métro line on boulevard de la Chapelle is full of rolls of colourful African fabrics as well as foodstuffs, although the shopping magnet here is the pink and white check awnings of Paris' most famous budget institution, Tati.

Pigalle to Batignolles

Down below the butte, Pigalle is still infamous for its sex shows and video shops, as well as cabaret survivor the Moulin Rouge; but there are also some oddities, such as the specialists in electric guitars along rue Douai. Stretching south of boulevard de Rochechouart and boulevard de Clichy, in the mid-19th century, the area known as the Nouvelle Athènes drew writers, artists and composers, among them Chopin and George Sand, as well as actresses and courtesans. The houses on place St-Georges, the Musée Gustave Moreau and

Above: Sacré Coeur. Below: art nouveau influence on the Métro.

Musée de la Vie Romantique or the exclusive private residential streets or 'villas' off rue des Martyrs give an idea of its rather grander past. Rue Clauzel is an enclave of retro clothing outlets, bric-a-brac and boho clothes shops, including sister act Hortensia Louisor; while the lower half of rue des Martyrs has several good bakeries and delis. An area that was fashionable in the 19th century and is gradually being rediscovered today.

West of Place de Clichy, the area of Batignolles grew up in the 19th century with a very different atmosphere to that of the grand mansions and apartment blocks of the western half of the 17th *arrondissement* around Parc Monceau. Sliced through by a huge area of railway depots that are due to be redeveloped, it still retains its authentic urban fabric, with old working-class cafés, budget hotels, craft workshops and picturesque alleys and courtyards, but it is increasingly being colonised by quirky boutiques and arty bistros.

Fashion & Footwear

Bonnie Cox
38 rue des Abbesses, 18th [B2]
Tel: 01 42 54 95 68
Bonnie Cox is one of the longer-standing Abbesses addresses and reputed for its pick of streetwise casual wear.

La Citadelle
3 rue des Trois-Frères, 18th [C2]
Tel: 01 42 52 21 56
The well-chosen selection of womenswear is a bit more grown-up than some of the more radical stuff in the area. Look out for delicate tops, linen trousers, flowing embroidered skirts and floaty dresses all arranged by colour.

Emmanuelle Zysman
81 rue des Martyrs, 18th [C3]
Tel: 01 42 52 01 00
Zysman's witty bags and purses stand out thanks to her tongue-in-cheek use of images from colonial advertising and vintage postcards. There's also jewellery and a small clothing collection, including her own T-shirts. Closed Monday.

FuturWare Lab
23 rue Houdon, 18th [B3]
Tel: 01 42 23 66 08
Russian Tatiana Lebedev studied fine art and theatre design in Moscow and has previously designed costumes for the Comédie Française – something that shows in her futuristic wear.

Street signs and purchases from bargain Montmartre institution, Tati.

Expect ingenious layering, transformable dresses and hi-tech fabrics.

Heaven
83 rue des Martyrs, 18th [C3]
Tel: 01 44 92 92 92
In this boutique-cum-workshop, English designer Lea-Anne Wallis makes and sells her appealing and varied designs, ranging from sober denim or linen trousers to neo-Pop blouses, ruffle skirts and vibrant long, strapless raw silk dress. Funky lamps, too. Closed Monday.

Hortensia Louisor
14 rue Clauzel, 9th [B3]
Tel: 01 45 26 67 68
Dresses for women and children using African prints and batiks give Caroline and Monique Louisor's designs a more summery tropical feel than their sister Patricia *(see below)*, reflecting their origins in Martinique. Closed Monday morning.

Patricia Louisor
16 rue Houdon, 18th [B3]
Tel: 01 42 62 10 42
Patricia Louisor has lots of fans of her well-priced, original clothing. The range is small and changes often, but expect floor-dragging skirts and wide trousers, with clever colour highlights or zip details.

Spree
16 rue La Vieuville, 18th [C2]
Tel: 01 42 23 41 40
In a distinctly Montmartre take on the concept store, this long, white space combines art and photography exhibitions with a chilled-out selection of adventurous clothes (think T-shirts and dirty denim), accessories and a miscellany of notebooks, CDs and 1960s' furniture. Closed Monday and August.

Têtes en l'Air
65 rue des Abbesses, 18th [B2]
Tel: 01 46 06 71 19
Top off your outfit with an outlandish piece of headgear at this

Flamboyant hats at Têtes en l'Air.

small *atelier*-boutique where hats can be made to measure. Novelties spotted here include a Christmas tree hat and a bird-in-a-cage hat.

Jewellery/Accessories

Black & Kausel
Galerie 45 rue Lepic, 18th [B2] Tel: 01 42 54 12 16
This shop sells unusual contemporary jewellery by a range of international designers, all displayed in changing exhibitions, along with selected art works. Closed mornings and all day Monday.

Jérémie Barthod
7 rue des Trois-Frères, 18th [C2] Tel: 01 42 62 54 50
The signature feature of Barthod's distinctive costume jewellery is a fine, wire coil, with silver, gold or bronze finish, that can appear either unadorned in simple minimalist necklaces and snaky bracelets or combined with resin beads or flower buds.

Health & Beauty

Détaille
10 rue St-Lazare, 9th [South of B3] Tel: 01 40 16 95 95

Neither the decor nor the stock seem to have changed much here over the past century. The old-fashioned wood panelling is intact, and the shelves are stacked with toilet waters such as *Eau de Fontaine*, *Eau Douce*, and bottles bearing names including *Shéhane* and *Alisée*. You'll even find the *Baume Automobile*, a cream invented for the Comtesse de Presles, an early motoring pioneer.

Departments Stores

Tati
4 boulevard Rochechouart, 18th [D3] Tel: 01 55 29 50 00
Every bit as much a Paris institution at the budget end of the market as department stores Printemps and Galeries Lafayette are at the top, Tati has to be experienced to be believed. The store, which sprawls along the boulevard, resembles a seige as women rummage through the boxes for tights and T-shirts at remarkably low prices, or even a polyester wedding dress. You'll also find menswear, table linen, beauty products, lingerie and related shops of sweets and jewellery.

Did you know?
Montmartre has its own vineyard. It was planted in 1933 in memory of the vineyards that once covered the hill. The grapes are harvested every October, then pressed and matured at the town hall. The wine, which has been described as the 'most expensive bad wine in the world' is later auctioned off for charity.

Listings

Right: Rare vinyl records at Dub Wize. Far right: Affordable wines from Caves des Abesses.

Design & Interiors

La Compagnie Colons
14 rue Clauzel, 9th [B3]
tel: 01 53 21 05 72
Stocks a well-chosen selection of ethnic design, mainly from Africa. There are chunky wooden mirrors and photo frames, cushions, rugs, small items of furniture, bags and necklaces. Lots of good gift ideas.

Novitas
19 rue La Vieuville, 18th [C2]
Tel: 01 42 23 22 87
Dedicated to the clean lines and ingenious ideas of modern design, this boutique focuses mainly on Scandinavian designers, including Holger Strom lights and plenty of stainless steel items from Arne Jacobsen and Erik Magnusson.

Books & Music

Centrale Guitars
8–12 rue de Douai, 9th [B3]
Tel: 01 42 81 13 15
This street is almost entirely devoted to the cult of the guitar, and Centrale Guitars has perhaps the biggest selection. It stocks acoustic, electric and bass guitars, amplifiers and accessories, from budget models to vintage items – Fenders and Gibsons.

Dub Wize
60 rue Hermel, 18th [C1]
Tel: 01 46 06 01 03
DJs cross town to root for reggae, ragga and dub records at Dub Wize. As well as CDs, there's a good selection of vinyl LPs and rare 45s. Closed mornings. Open Sunday afternoon.

Children

Gaspard de la Butte
10bis rue Yvonne-Le-Tac, 18th [C2] Tel: 01 42 55 99 40
Original clothing for 0 to 6 year olds – from floral dresses to crisp twill trousers and floppy sunhats – is made up at the back of the shop.

Merci Maman
73 place du Dr-Félix-Lobligeois, [west of A2] 17th
Tel: 01 42 29 11 62
An upmarket and imaginative, but unpretentious, selection of clothes for babies and children (up to around age 8) includes Antik Batik, Jean Bourget, IKKS, Lili Gaufrette and Contre Vents et Marées.

Food & Drink

Caves des Abbesses
43 rue des Abbesses, 18th [B2]
Tel: 01 42 52 81 54

Among the food shops and cafés along rue des Abbesses, this wine shop puts the emphasis on affordable wines from small producers. At the back, with a roaring fire in winter, is a tiny, cheery wine bar, where you can try out different wines along with plates of cheese and cold cuts.

Fromagerie de Montmartre
9 rue de Poteau, 18th [C1]
Tel: 01 46 06 26 03
In this pretty vintage cheese shop on a food-obsessed street near the Mairie du XVIIIe, a fine selection of cheeses are laid out on pristine straw-covered racks.

Specialist

Dreyfus
2 rue Charles-Nodier, 18th [C2]
Tel: 01 46 06 92 25
Much loved by decorators and fashion designers, Dreyfus is the largest of the fabric merchants who congregate around the Marché St-Pierre and along rue d'Orsel. Five floors burst with a colossal choice, including some great bargains on discounted bolts. Closed Monday.

Retro boutiques
Retro style has become highly collectable in Paris, and the Montmartre area offers a couple of excellent dealers. At **Pages 50/70** *(15 rue Yvonne Le Tac, tel: 01 42 52 48 59)*, Olivier Verlet specialises in ceramics and glassware by French and Italian designers with streamlined shapes or anamorphic forms, but also has some furniture and lighting. **Galerie Christine Diegoni** *(47ter rue d'Orsel, tel: 01 42 64 69 48)* features furniture from names such as Charles Eames, Florence Knoll and George Nelson.

Tam Tam
20 rue Yvonne-le-Tac, 18th [C2]
Tel: 01 42 54 54 96
A treasure trove of African and Middle Eastern jewellery and tribal art includes fabulous antique Yemenite necklaces and rings, Indian bracelets, Touare rings, striking African glass bead headdresses and wooden stools picked up on the owner's voyages.

WHERE TO UNWIND

La Fourmi
74 rue des Martyrs, 18th [C3] Tel: 01 42 64 70 35. This buzzy designer café on a busy Pigalle corner is a convenient spot for checking out the clothes designers on rue des Martyrs.

Au Grain de Folie
24 rue de La Vieuville,18th [C2] Tel: 01 42 58 15 57. This tiny restaurant just off place des Abbesses is one of the oldest of Paris's scarce vegetarian eateries. There's a small choice of soups, salads, stews and organic wines.

Aux Négociants
27 rue Lambert, 18th [C2] Tel: 01 46 06 15 11 A simple, rustic wine bar/bistro. Try one of the well-prepared *plats du jour* with a wine from the Beaujolais region. The real thing.

Le Relais Gascon
6 rue des Abbesses, 18th [B2] Tel: 01 42 58 58 22. Long serving hours and low prices make this busy bistro a good choice when you're on a shopping trawl. Their speciality is *salades géantes* served in big earthenware bowls.

Le Sancerre
35 rue des Abbesses, 18th [B2] Tel: 01 42 58 47 05. This is the must-visit café on rue des Abbesses, drawing an eclectic, young, arty crowd. Good salads and wines, and pavement chairs to allow you to enjoy the scene.

MARKETS

Paris's numerous markets, whether upmarket, tatty, daily or weekly, pull in bargain hunters, gourmets and collectors alike

Map on Inside Front Cover

FLEA MARKETS

The fleamarkets of Paris developed in the 19th-century, as *ferrailleurs* (scrap-metal merchants) and *chiffonniers* (rag-and-bone men) camped in the unbuilt zone just outside the Thiers fortifications. They made their living from the debris of the Paris population, avoiding the duties within the city walls.

Marché de St-Ouen

The **Puces de St-Ouen** (often referred to as the Puces de Clignancourt) in the north of Paris is the big giant. There are over 2,500 dealers grouped in over a dozen individual markets and arcades, most of them opening off rue de Rosiers. You can spend days making your way round the numerous stalls – St-Ouen has an enormous range of specialists and something for everybody. Although a few of the markets remain shabby, and some hopefuls still try to sell clapped-out junk on the ground in the backstreets, much of what is on sale is classy and often quite pricey, many of the stalls have the allure of shops, and stallholders are knowledgeable enthusiasts. While some bargaining is part of the game, this is not a souk – you'll rarely get a price down by more than 10 or 15 percent. Stallholders accept cheques – and maybe even credit cards – and they should provide written receipts. Transporters and shipping facilities are available, should your purchase be too big to carry. The market is open Saturday, Sunday and Monday; Mondays are quieter, with fewer stalls.

Opposite and below: antiques and bric-a-brac at the Marché de St-Ouen.

The Puces de St-Ouen has recently been listed as an historic monument in an attempt to preserve its character – and perhaps also to remind Parisians of its existence (an estimated 80 percent of visitors are foreigners). Note that crowds can be dense, especially under the Périphérique and at the junction of rue des Rosiers and avenue Michelet.

Opened in 1920, **Marché Vernaisson** (99 rue des Rosiers) is one of the longest established and most characterful of Paris's markets; it is held over a maze of alleys running between rue des Rosiers and avenue Michelet, and many stallholders have been here for generations. Goods range from Dinky cars, toy trains, lead animals and dolls-house furniture to Art Deco lights, assorted furniture, silverware and cutlery.

Nearby, two parallel alleyways at **Marché Biron** (85 rue des Rosiers) feature lots of Napoléon III furniture. Here, there are also specialists in fans, Lalique glass, chandeliers and vintage posters.

Across the street, **Marché Malassis** (142 rue des Rosiers) is a modern markets on two floors. An eclectic range of dealers trade in toy cars, Disney memorabilia, watches, vintage cameras, perfume

bottles, couture, North African furniture and carpets, 20th-century design, pens and office equipment and Lalique glass.

Next door, **Marché Dauphine** (138–40 rue des Rosiers) is the most recent of the markets at St-Ouen, opened in 1991, in a two-storey purpose-built building complete with escalators. Among 300 dealers, there are specialists in Bentwood furniture, Biedermeier, art nouveau and art deco, Japanese and Chinese art, oil paintings and mirrors, ornate 19th-century glazed earthenware, vintage couture and accessories, scientific instruments, cameras, books and prints, and rustic dressers.

Marché Serpette (110 rue des Rosiers) is grand with a nucleus of dealers specialising in art deco furniture and cocktail sets but beware – a lot is over-restored. Other stalls include costume-jewellery specialist, Olwen Forrest, and the Monde du Baggage, with its vintage Hermès and Vuitton luggage.

Running in an L-shape around the outside of **Marché Paul Bert** (104 rue des Rosiers), a good source of vintage garden furniture and outdoor statuary, is a great array of bric-a-brac and antiques. Bachelier Antiquités draws dealers and collectors for its beautiful, if not cheap, vintage kitchenware, while Vingtième Siècle features cult 1950s to 1970s furniture design from style-conscious manufacturer Knoll et al.

If many of the stalls at St-Ouen today resemble smart antique shops – some also have smart addresses within Paris – the glass-roofed, galleried **Marché Jules Vallès** (7 rue Jules Vallès) remains closer to the true flea-market spirit with its mish-mash of furniture, ceramics, ironwork, lighting and kitsch. It can be a place for finds for those in the know. Even more reminiscent of a fleamarket is the **Marché Vallès Lecuyer** (between rue Jules Vallès and rue Lecuyer), where a lot of the furniture, vintage radios and boxes of books on sale is in poor condition.

Running alongside the Périphérique, the **Marché Malik** (59 rue Jean-Henri Fabre) is the traditional place to find second-hand clothes. Although a few dealers stocking genuine vintage gear remain, it has become increasingly dominated by stalls of discount clothing and leather jackets, as well as a few young designers, joining up with the clothes stalls that stretch towards Porte de Clignancourt Métro station.

Marché de Montreuil

Tattier and far more anarchic than St-Ouen, Montreuil (Avenue de la Porte de Montreuil, Métro Porte de Montreuil) is a fleamarket where 'flea' is still the operative word. Stalls packed into a triangle of land between the Périphérique and this eastern suburb are heavy on unidentifiable car parts and tools, broken chairs and lots of unwashed clothes. Expect piles of grubby jeans, new discount wares, stacks of socks and underwear, bed and household linen, and a mishmash of bric-a-brac and collectables, mainly from the 20th century. Collectors typically hunt out items such as *pastis* jugs and memorabilia, telephone cards and old hats, but if you're lucky you might find Limoges porcelain or interesting wine gadgets among the clutter. A smaller section, further along the railway tracks has more furniture and decorative items. The market is open Saturday, Sunday and Monday.

Marché de Vanves

Open only on Saturday and Sunday and smaller than St-Ouen or Montreuil, Vanves (Avenue de la Porte de Vanves, Métro Porte de Vanves) is a relaxed easygoing fleamarket just within the Périphérique ringroad. Come in the morning, as many of the stalls pack up in mid-afternoon. You won't find major antiques here, but it is a good source of old lace and table linen, all sorts of ceramic bibelots and ornaments, costume jewellery, old postcards and magazines, tins and children's toys, and some furniture.

Marché d'Aligre

Situated on the square next to the rue d'Aligre food market, this is the oldest fleamarket in Paris and the only one within the city boundary. A handful of outdoor stalls charge what generally seem like astronomically optimistic prices for costume jewellery, old china, cutlery, paintings, books and prints and a considerable amount of junk. Finds are occasionally made, in particular among the books and drawings. Open Tuesday to Sunday mornings.

Opposite and above: From artworks and furniture to chess and kitchenware, there's plenty to peruse, but come early for the best bargains.

FOOD MARKETS

Food is an essential part of French culture, and Paris's food markets remain a vital ingredient of life in the capital. A reminder that this city is lived in, even in the centre, is the fact that most residents still prefer to shop where possible at the local market.

Roving Markets

It's at the 'roving' street markets that pop up two or three mornings a week (7am–2.30pm) all over town that you'll often find the most authentic produce and a true local flavour that varies from *quartier* to *quartier*. At weekends in particular, the market is as much a local rendez-vous for bumping into friends and exchanging gossip as for stocking up on provisions. Today, there are over 50 street markets in Paris; some consist of just a handful of stalls, others, such as **Marché Bastille** or **avenue Daumesnil**, stretch for hundreds of metres and have outstanding ranges of produce. Some stalls appear at different markets on different days. As well as lots of general butchers, fishmongers, fabulous cheese stalls and greengrocers, you'll find specialists – perhaps a stall entirely devoted to onions and shallots, another to varieties of lettuce or to Breton cakes. A surprising number of *maraichers* (where you are buying direct from producers) are a reminder that market gardening and fruit production are still active, even in the surrounding Ile de France region and nearby Picardy. As well as food and flowers, most markets also have a number of household stalls, where you'll find kitchen equipment, inexpensive clothing or leather goods.

Look out in particular for seasonal produce: in spring it could be a glut of asparagus, in winter impressive mounds of cep mushrooms or the fur and feathers of wild game. And, depending on the season, there are often hot dishes that can be picked up that would be good for a picnic or a snack: rows of spit-roast chickens, iron platters of paella, big vats of steaming choucroute or thin Lebanese pizzas.

Among specific markets, in the Latin Quarter, **Place Monge** is particularly animated on Sunday morning when it is less touristy than nearby rue Mouffetard, and, though quite small, it has good specialist stalls in apples from Picardy, Alpine hams and cheeses, a recommended wine merchant, Caribbean and Middle Eastern snacks and a stall with honey and homemade jams and cakes. Several of the same stalls crop up at **Port-Royal**, which spreads out along the boulevard in the shadow of the Val de Grâce hospital.

Place Maubert has a higher proportion of general goods and clothes stalls than most markets, including African sculptures, handbags and luggage, as well as stalls of Southwestern French food products and olive oil.

Across the river, east of Bastille, **Rue d'Aligre**, which draws a large North African contingent both as stallholders and customers, is renowned for selling some of the best and cheapest vegetables in Paris, especially if you arrive at the end of the morning when stallholders sell off courgettes, potatoes, fresh herbs, etc in vast quantities.

Stretching along the broad road of the same name east of Nation, the **Cours de Vincennes** has plenty of vegetables and tempting roast chicken, any number of fishmongers, plus stalls of kitchen utensils and inexpensive shirts and clothing. **Barbès market**, held underneath the overhead Métro along boulevard de la Chapelle, is renowned for African products, from exotic fruit to rolls of colourful cloth. **Boulevard de Belleville** is another ethnically diverse area, while the small market on

WHERE AND WHEN

The following is a list of selected addresses, given by *arrondissement*. For a full list of Parisian markets, visit www.mairie-paris.fr.

Place Baudoyer, 4th. Métro Pont-Marie. Wed 4–8pm and Sat morning.

Place Maubert, 5th. Métro Maubert-Mutualité. Tues, Thur and Sat morning.

Place Monge, 5th. Métro Place Monge. Wed, Fri and Sun morning.

Boulevard de Port Royal, 5th. RER Port-Royal. Tues, Thur and Sat morning.

Boulevard Raspail (between rue du Cherche-Midi and rue de Rennes), 6th. Métro Rennes. Organic market Sun morning; general market Tues and Fri.

Saxe-Breteuil, avenue du Saxe, 7th. Métro Ségur. Thur and Sat morning.

Boulevard de Batignolles, 8th. Métro Rome. Organic market Sat morning.

Bastille, boulevard Richard-Lenoir (between rue Amelot and rue St-Sabin), 11th. Métro Bastille. Thur and Sun morning.

Boulevard de Belleville, 11th. Métro Belleville. Tues and Fri morning.

Rue d'Aligre, 12th. Métro Ledru-Rollin. Tues–Sun morning (plus covered market Beauvau-St-Antoine, morning and afternoon).

Cours de Vincennes, 12th. Métro Nation. Wed and Sat morning.

Daumesnil, avenue Daumesnil (between place Félix-Eboué and rue de Charenton), 12th. Métro Daumesnil or Dugommier. Tues and Fri morning.

Boulevard Auguste-Blanqui, 13th. Métro Place d'Italie/Corvisart. Tues, Fri and Sun morning.

Boulevard Edgar-Quinet, 14th. Métro Edgar-Quinet. Weds and Sat morning.

Rue de la Convention, 15th. Métro Convention. Tues, Thur and Sun morning.

Boulevard de Grenelle (between rue Lourmel and rue du Commerce), 15th. Métro La Motte-Piquet-Grenelle. Wed and Sun morning.

Avenue du Président-Wilson, 16th. Métro Alma-Marceau or Iéna. Wed and Sat morning.

Rue La Fontaine, 16th. Métro Ranelagh. Tues and Fri morning.

Barbès, boulevard de la Chapelle, 18th. Métro Barbès-Rochechouart. Wed and Sat morning.

Rue Joinville, 19th. Métro Crimée. Thur and Sun morning.

Place des Fêtes, 19th. Métro Place des Fêtes. Tues, Fri and Sun morning.

Rue des Pyrénées, 20th. Métro Pyrénées. Thur and Sun morning.

There's a quite different character in smart western Paris – **Rue Fontaine** is a small but classy street market that climbs up behind the circular Maison de la Radio, past some of Hector Guimard's celebrated art nouveau apartment blocks. In **avenue du Président-Wilson** and **avenue du Saxe-Breteuil**, upmarket produce and an equally chic clientele are set off by stunning views of the Eiffel Tower. The good-quality produce of both stalls and surrounding food shops on rue de la Convention reflects the foodie preoccupations of this residential and generally tourist-free area.

Although most roving markets are morning-only, in a recent sign of adaptation to the working lifestyle, the **place Baudroyer market**, near the Hôtel de Ville, opens on Wednesday evening (4–8pm), an experiment that may be taken up elsewhere.

Another growth area is in organic produce featured at the **Marchés Biologiques**. The best-known and longest-established market of this type is the **Marché Biologique Raspail**, which draws a chic crowd from all over Paris every Sunday morning; there's also an organic market at **Batignolles** on Saturday morning. As everywhere with organic products, quality is generally high, but prices are far from rustic. And although principally dominated by food and wine, you'll also find assorted organic or natural products, such as cleaning products and natural clothes.

TIP

If you're interested in antiques and collectables, look out also for the *brocantes* held around Paris over a few days or a weekend, and generally publicised by posters and banners in the streets. They sell furniture, ceramics, jewellery, prints and postcards, etc. and are often cheaper than the flea-markets as many dealers come from out of town and are keen to shift material.

Market Streets

Food shops with stalls that spill out onto the pavement are generally open Tuesday to Saturday all day, with (be warned) a very long break for lunch, and on Sunday morning. Perhaps the best known and full of character, even if it draws as many tourists as it does residents, is that on **rue Mouffetard** (5th) in the Latin Quarter, which winds its way down one of the oldest streets in Paris towards place St-Médard. Look out for the Italian deli Facchetti and Steff the baker.

Pedestrianised **rue Daguerre** is a real focus of local life in the 14th *arrondissement*, with two very good cheese shops (Vacroux and Androuët) and a good fishmonger, as well as several thriving cafés.

Rue Montorgueil (1st) is a reminder of the wholesale market that used to exist nearby at Les Halles with a youthful crowd throng the pavement cafés amid wine merchants, fruit stalls and lovely vintage patisserie Stohrer.

Rue Cler (7th) is an upmarket haunt with good delis, fine hams and cheeses, and an ever-packed café terrace at the Cafe du Marché. Near Ternes, **rue Poncelet** (17th) is a good place to buy fish, you'll find aromatic fresh-roasting coffee at the Brûlerie des Ternes, German cakes at the Le Stubbli and fine cheeses at Alléosse, while **rue Lévis** (also in the 17th), on the edge of Batignolles, has a more local, working atmosphere.

Covered Markets

Paris's most famous covered market used to be the central Les Halles wholesale fruit and vegetable market – the Parisian equivalent of London's Covent Garden – with its elaborate cast-iron market pavilions. The building was demolished in 1969 when the market was moved out of town to Rungis *(see pp47–9)*. However, the cast-iron building boom that took place during the 19th century also sparked the construction of covered local markets around the growing city, and a dozen examples from that period and later still survive.

The best-preserved and most-authentic of these cast-iron covered markets is the **Marché St-Quentin** (85 boulevard Magenta, 10th), built in the 1880s. The market remains a thriving hub of activity, with a range of stalls selling fresh produce and exotic snacks and a convivial café situated handily in the middle. Nearby is **Marché St-Martin** (31 rue du Château d'Eau, 10th), although this is a much more modern construction.

The cast-iron **Marché Beauvais-Antoine** (12th) adjoins the street market along rue d'Aligre but it sells pricier, generally complementary produce. The indoor market is good for cheese, fish and wine, while the area outdoors is better for fruit and vegetables.

The 1950s' **Marché Passy**, in the 16th, is home to a series of twee huts, but there are good cut meats and fresh pasta available here. The covered **Marché St-Germain** (6th) occupies what has been a fair and

market place ever since the Middle Ages, but redevelopment in the 1990s turned most of the building into a shopping centre/swimming pool/concert hall complex and only a handful of stalls remain. Likewise up for redevelopment was the historic **Marché des Enfants-Rouge** (3rd) on rue de Bretagne in the Marais, which was saved from closure but has yet to fully recover from rebuilding.

Like the market streets, the covered markets usually open Tuesday to Saturday all day (with a long break for lunch) and on Sunday morning.

Most market streets open all day (but with a long lunch break) from Tuesday to Saturday, and on Sunday morning.

ESSENTIAL INFORMATION

Money Matters

Banks in France usually open from 9am–5pm, Monday–Friday; some close for lunch from 12.30–2.30pm. All banks shut on public holidays, often from 12pm on the previous day. The majority of cashpoint machines (ATMs) accept all major debit and credit cards with a 'PIN' number. Most shops and restaurants accept all major cards.

Opening Hours

Shops usually open from 9 or 10am until around 7pm, although food shops (*boulangeries*, etc.) open earlier. Few stores open on Sunday, except those in the Marais and one or two on the Champs-Elysées. Some smaller shops close on Monday all day or in the morning until 2pm, and throughout August for their annual holiday.

Public Holidays

1 January, Easter Monday, 1 May, 8 May, Ascension Day, Whit Monday, 14 July, 15 August, 1 November; 11 November, 25 December.

Public Transport

The **Métro** runs from 5.30am to about 12.30am, its lines identified by numbers, colours and the names of terminals (see map on inside back cover). The Métro runs in conjunction with the **RER** (suburban regional express trains). There are five main RER lines (A, B, C, D, E), and the trains run every 12 minutes from 5.30am to 12am. Most **buses** run from 6.30am to 8.30pm, with some continuing until 12.30am. Route maps can be found posted inside buses and at bus stops.

The same tickets are valid for use on the Métro, RER and bus systems. Singles, returns and multiple-ticket 'carnets' are available from stations and some *tabacs* (tobacconists). Bus tickets may also be purchased from the driver.

Sales

The two main sales (*soldes*) periods in France are January and July.

Size conversions

Women: 38 (UK 8/US 6), 40 (UK 10/US 8), 42 (UK 12/US 10), etc. Men's suits: just subtract 10 eg French 46 is a UK or US 36. Men's shirts: 36 (14 UK/US), 37 (14½) 38 (15) etc.

Telephones and internet

Most public phone boxes in Paris are card-operated. Phone-cards or *télécartes* can be bought from kiosks, tobacconist's and post offices. **Emergency numbers**: ambulance 15; fire dpt 18; police 17; emergencies from a mobile 112. SOS Help (English helpline, 3–11pm daily): 01 47 23 80 80. There are numerous **internet cafés** around the city centre. The Virgin Megastore's cyber café stays open until midnight *(see p26)*. The Champs-Elysées branch of easyEverything is open 24-hours. **Useful websites** include: www.magicparis.com for information on travel, shops, hotels, etc; www.pariscope.fr, the weekly listings magazine online; www.pagesjaunes.com, the French yellow pages; www.ratp.fr. for information on public transport and www.paris-touristoffice.com.

Tourist Information

The main Paris tourist office is at 127 avenue des Champs-Elysées, 8th (open daily 9am–8pm), with branches at the Gare de Lyon and by the Eiffel Tower. For entertainment listings, the weekly magazine *Pariscope* is issued every Wednesday with a section in English.

Value-Added Tax

On most purchases the price includes VAT (TVA in French). Foreign visitors can claim this back, but only if you spend more than 640 euros (300 euros for EU citizens) in one shop. The store should give you a *bordereau* (export sales invoice), which you'll need to fill in and show, with the goods, to customs officials. You then send the form back to the retailer, who will refund the VAT.

SHOPS A–Z

The following is a complete list of the shops reviewed in this guide.
For details of other branches, refer to the main entry; where these are too
numerous to list in full, a telephone number is given through which you
should be able to find out address details.

Fashion & Footwear

Jewellery, Accessories & Watches

Health & Beauty

Department Stores

Design & Interiors

Art & Antiques

Sport & Leisure

Specialist

Acknowledgments
The publishers would like to thank all stores kind enough to allow us to photograph on their premises.